WHEN MUM AND DAD SEE ME KICK

WHEN MUM AND DAD SEE ME KICK

STUART THOMAS

FAIRPLAY
PUBLISHING

First published in 2023 by Fair Play Publishing
PO Box 4101, Balgowlah Heights, NSW 2093, Australia
www.fairplaypublishing.com.au

ISBN: 978-1-925914-60-3

ISBN: 978-1-925914-61-0 (ePub)

© Stuart Thomas 2023

The moral rights of the author have been asserted.

All rights reserved. Except as permitted under the *Australian Copyright Act 1968* (for example, a fair dealing for the purposes of study, research, criticism or review), no part of this book may be reproduced, stored in a retrieval system, communicated or transmitted in any form or by any means without prior written permission from the Publisher.

Cover design and Typesetting by Leslie Priestley

All inquiries should be made to the Publisher via sales@fairplaypublishing.com.au

NATIONAL
LIBRARY
OF AUSTRALIA

A catalogue record of this book is available from the National Library of Australia.

CONTENTS

INTRODUCTION	1
TILLY, AGE 6	6
CHARLIE, AGE 64	11
ISABELLA, AGE 17	21
ALI, AGE 48	31
JOHNNY, AGE 56	39
CARLA, AGE 24	52
TRAVIS, AGE 28	61
JULIETTE, AGE 32	72
GRAHAM, AGE 52	85
STUART, AGE 48	99
ACKNOWLEDGEMENTS	115
ABOUT THE AUTHOR	117

INTRODUCTION

My mother told me at a very young age to never discuss religion or politics in public. Subsequently, I have failed miserably in following that advice and discovered that there were potentially a few other topics she should also have included in her warning.

One would be football.

Often labelled the game of opinions, it is doubtful that any other physical activity has incited more passionate argument, discussion and discourse than the simple kicking of a sphere between two groups of 11 humans. At the elite level, that takes the form of disputed goals in major tournaments, claimed illegalities that have robbed entire countries of what they felt rightfully deserving of, and endless debate around the qualities of individual players and who has a claim to football superiority. Of course, for all of the above, there will simply never be a definitive and universally agreed view that settles discussion and calms the waters.

Such is the game of football.

Away from the cut and thrust of the professional game, conjecture also exists. Parents grapple with a perception that their child is not receiving the same opportunities as others, youth representative selection is fraught with drama and dispute, and referees still exist in a world where the level of respect shown towards them falls well short of the ideal and what simply should be expected.

The game extracts passion from all those involved with it, encouraging the vocalisation of frustration, disappointment and triumph, with the person standing nearby almost certain to be holding a diametrically opposed point of view.

It is that difference of opinion that fuels the game and the continued commitment to it shared by billions of fans around the globe.

Perhaps the most important component of the dynamic is the unique and personal perspectives that people bring to the game. No two are the same, with football lenses based on distinct and individual experiences that shape the way the game is interpreted.

For decades, that uniqueness has fascinated me.

In social interactions with players, coaches, administrators, media types and general supporters across many years, where people often have attempted to claim some sort of higher ground based on their knowledge of and/or participation in the game, it always struck me that they were somewhat missing the point.

I have chatted with ex-players determined to remind me just how good they were, been shown coaching qualifications framed on walls by junior coaches, heard kids belittle others based on their lesser skills and frequently been spoken down to by people evidently convinced that they know just that little bit more about the game than me.

As such a vast entity, football contains an enormous number of contentious issues around which discussion takes place. Whether it be VAR, referees, competition structures, youth development or the best players, teams and moments, it seems many take the myriad content available as a means by which they can argumentatively prove themselves as being a little bit more football than the next person.

In fact, the majority of the issues up for debate are almost certainly hazy and malleable, with very little in football hard, fast and indisputable.

As a result, football means a lot of different things to different people. Some attend matches to get drunk and start fights with opposition supporters. Others are obsessed with coaching young players and encouraging them to become the best possible, whilst many fans of the game simply sit back and admire the skill, dexterity and class that makes football almost balletic at times.

However, not only do fans of the game give to it emotionally and physically, every one of them takes something from it, whether they may be conscious of the fact or not. As potentially the most perfect metaphor for humanity, football educates us all on a social and cultural level. Experiences in the game are educative, with the lessons taken from it sometimes life-changing, yet always meaningful.

It was that idea that nurtured this book.

As a well-known chatterbox and someone holding a belief that relationships and communication lie at the absolute core of growth, opportunity and contentedness, I have spent countless hours speaking with and listening to people involved in football.

Their stories fascinate me and reinforce a view that sport can play a powerful role in people's journeys, often as a calming counterbalance to lives filled with so much that is ultimately pointless and meaningless.

There was no need to set out and do any interviewing or substantial research to inform the book. I had already completed the bulk of it, unaware that what I had in fact been doing in all the conversations that had taken place over the years was cataloguing the footballing lives of a group of people who had been touched and deeply affected by their experiences in the game.

Some of the subjects are no longer with us, others I have had no contact with for years, whilst a few are more immediate and contemporary. The notion of telling their stories was appealing, yet discovering the means by which to do so challenging.

Using an interview, question and answer style seemed clunky and fraught with guesswork, especially considering the impossibility of recalling precisely what I had asked someone 15 years ago amidst conversation. Instead, the use of the first person seemed to lend itself more to the project.

With permission granted from the subjects where available, I set about writing as them, in personal narrative voices and in an attempt to take the reader on a journey through their time in the game—what it meant to them, took from them and provided.

Whether I have done it successfully will be for someone else to decide.

Tilly, age 6, conveys the thoughts of a young local player whom I had the pleasure of meeting as she began her football journey. Tilly's parents were so accommodating in allowing me to attempt to look inside the sheer innocence and excitement of a child engaging with the game for the first time.

Charlie's story is of a proud Noongar man, age 64, whom I met in 2003, and with whom I shared plenty of pints and an entire afternoon in the warm Western Australian sun at a local beer garden. Ali, age 48, is the same age as me and a boy against whom I played football in the 1980s. His story was tough to write at times, with personal memories of what he faced as a disabled player in a far less accommodating time still vivid.

Isabella, age 17, is a young girl whose playing career I have followed after befriending her mother the very first day we became next-door neighbours. Carla, age 25, is a cousin, whose relationship with her father developed further thanks to football, and Juliette, age 32, is a young woman I met in 2020, keen to talk about some of the most complex and important issues when it comes to sport, gender, diversity and inclusion.

Travis, age 28, is one of my favourite subjects, a player on the long road back from serious injury, and the refereeing stories relayed by Graham, age 52, had me in stitches. Hopefully the story of Johnny, age 56, moves your soul as it did mine—a wonderful man I knew many years ago and someone now missed by many.

There are moments where I struggled to recapture the voice of the subject to my satisfaction, with the effort to do so and subsequently do justice to their experiences paramount in my thinking. Hopefully, they read well and move readers in much the same way they did me when I first listened to them speak.

Each story enunciates just how powerful football can be and the potentially positive role it can play at both the individual and community levels. Perhaps its healing forces and ability to encourage and engender good have never been more important than right now, as the world continues to grapple with horrifying injustice, aggression and the bigotry that holds humanity back from what it could potentially be.

If the stories featured in this book prove anything at all, it is that no two individual experiences in football could ever be the same. I will be forever grateful to those who agreed to allow me to write openly about what are, at times, difficult experiences to recount and am particularly respectful of the lives and dignity of the now deceased people about whom stories have been written.

Knowing each of the subjects, some for just a brief period and others for a lifetime, has added pleasure, knowledge and understanding to my own journey. Their stories moved me to tears, made me smile and confirmed a firmly held belief that as humans, we really do know very little about the people who stroll past us every day, or live behind that common wall on the left.

As a direct result of researching and writing these stories, significant personal reflection took place in terms of empathy and understanding.

In that spirit, it only felt responsible and apt to share my football journey, warts and all and including the bits and pieces that I probably never expected to see the light of day. In the process of doing so, I experienced a similar catharsis to that expressed by others whose stories I share; a wonderful sense of freedom and release in telling the story and also some darker moments where regret and sadness lurked around events that are usually locked away in a mental vault due to their uncomfortable nature.

If one of these stories strikes a chord with you, draws a tear, makes you laugh or merely forces a thought, I will be as pleased as punch. The next time someone jumps up on their soapbox and begins giving the impression that they may feel a little more football than you, think back to the subjects in this book.

My hope is that the gathering of the threads that form the fabrics of the subjects' lives will be a constant reminder to be a little less quick to judge, never too slow to empathise and to always remain aware that human beings' carry-on luggage can sometimes be astonishing and heartbreaking when explored.

Hopefully one day we will meet, and you can tell me your story.

Stuart Thomas
February 2023

TILLY, AGE 6

The first time Dad took me to the park to play soccer, it made me so happy. That was two years ago, and since then I have kicked a ball every single day. Even though we started saying football, we usually call it 'soccer' now because when I told the other kids at school that I was practising football with my dad they got confused about what I meant.

Every day after school I wait for him to come home from work. Mum goes crazy because I stand in the hallway near the front door, kicking a ball back and forth against the wall. There are a few marks there now, but, hopefully, I can keep hiding them with the coats that are on the back of the door.

The ball we use is a Chelsea FC one. It is blue and white with the Premier League logo on it. My grandfather was born in 1960 in London and went for that team when he was little. That is why Dad did too and why we always watch them play when they are on television.

When I first started kicking the ball I used to get very sore toes. Dad taught me how to turn my foot out and hit the ball with the inside part. It was so much easier and after a few weeks, I started to be able to kick with a lot more power.

I thought football was all about kicking the ball and not much else, but Dad showed me all the other skills you need to have as a player. I used to find it really hard to do throw-ins right; my stomach muscles would always hurt after practising them for a while.

Also, Dad got very frustrated when he tried to teach me to head the ball. Even though he was only doing little throws from about a metre away, I was too scared to let the ball hit my head. I always thought that my head was going to crack open. Eventually, I was brave enough and gave it a go. It hurts sometimes but when you use the right part of your head it actually feels pretty cool.

WHEN MUM AND DAD SEE ME KICK

Dad thought I might be able to become a really good goalkeeper because I was always pretty tall for my age. It didn't take long for him to change his mind because I kept dropping the ball every time he kicked it to me. I really respect the great goalkeepers we see on television, the way they throw their bodies at the ball and catch it easily when it is coming at them so quickly.

Even though I had played netball at school, catching a football that was speeding towards me was not fun or something I was very good at. Dad was smart to forget about me using my hands and focus on improving the foot skills that footballers need to be successful players.

One day Dad came home and put a note on the refrigerator. It was a call-out for girl football players from one of our local clubs. He told me to read the parts I could understand and ask about anything that didn't make sense. Then he asked whether I might be interested in playing real football.

I was so happy that I cried. Then I cuddled him and Mum.

We had to wait two months for the actual competition to start but filled in the online registration form straight away. I was surprised how much money it was going to cost. With the registration and team uniform together, Mum and Dad would be spending hundreds of dollars.

Sometimes I think parents don't realise that kids really do appreciate how much they spend on sports and activities. I know I do.

I bugged Dad even more to take me to the park after that and always sooked when it was time to leave. He could see how excited I was and we would kick for hours. Sometimes he got in trouble from Mum when we came home late and dinner was already on the table.

While we ate, all we talked about was soccer. I could tell that Mum was a little bored but she always asked me questions and tried to encourage me. Sometimes we would talk about the Matildas and my favourite player, Steph Catley. Steph plays left back and I want to play that position when I get older.

Playing as a left or right back means you get the chance to run up and down the wing and cross balls into the box for your strikers to score. It is a fun position but you have to make sure you turn around and run back to defend when the other team gets the ball.

A few weeks before the season began, I remember being at home one night when Dad said he had to go out and pick something up. I was lying on the lounge room floor and drawing a picture of Steph Catley for my art project at school. I'm not a very good drawer so it didn't really look like her.

Dad came back at around 7.30 p.m. and handed me a large paper bag. I didn't know what it was at first but reached in and pulled out some clothes. I realised quickly that it was a shirt and a matching pair of shorts. The shirt was yellow with brown stripes going up and down and the shorts were all brown.

When I held up the shirt, I saw the club logo of my new team and realised what the clothes were for.

Dad told me to reach deeper into the bag. I pulled out a matching pair of socks and two strange little pieces of plastic. I must have made a funny look on my face as Mum and Dad both burst out laughing when I held them up and asked what they were.

Mum said, "They are shin pads to protect your legs in case you get kicked: you put them inside your socks when you play."

I went into my room and put the entire uniform on, including the shin pads and then ran back into the lounge room. Mum started crying and saying all those silly things about her baby growing up and worrying that I might get hurt. To be honest, I kind of wanted to get hurt and all muddy and dirty from playing soccer.

I hugged them and then Dad said, "There is one more thing ... on Saturday. Boots!"

I'd never had a pair of football boots before and was worried that I might not be able to kick as well as I could in the runners that I wore at the park. Dad told me not to worry, and on Saturday morning we went to Rebel Warehouse to buy my first pair.

There were so many different colours and styles to choose from. There were pictures of famous footballers like Lionel Messi and Cristiano Ronaldo above the shoes and because there was a sale on, heaps of other kids and their parents were doing the same thing as us.

I tried on about four pairs and liked them all but there was a red pair of Adidas boots with three white stripes on the side that I really liked. Above the boots was a picture of Lionel Messi. Like millions of other kids, I really wanted to wear the same boots as him. I told Dad that it was meant to be.

He wouldn't let me wear them on the way home but we did go to the park straight away to try them out. I'll never forget the sound of that first kick in my new boots. It felt like I had more power, even though it took me a little while to get used to walking with those funny little bumps across the bottom.

I cleaned the boots with soapy water when I got home. I wanted them to look new forever.

Every few days I would put on my full team uniform with the boots and check myself out in front of the mirror. One day Mum walked in when I was doing the pose that Ronaldo does after he scores a goal.

She laughed and said, "I think you are gonna be good at this."

The club emailed and told us that training would be on Wednesdays at 5.30 p.m. Dad was going to take me when he got home from work at around five. I made sure I was dressed and ready so we would not be late, although we just made it on time for the first ever training day because I was all dressed up in my uniform when Dad got home.

He told me, "Sweetheart, the uniform is only for the games, you wear whatever you want to training."

Our coach is Rueben. He is a very nice man who never shouts at us if we make mistakes. He is really tall and has a weird accent that sometimes makes us laugh. Dad told me he is from Spain and that he was once a very good footballer when he was young. Sometimes when we take a break to have a drink at training, Rueben kicks the ball on his own and does a few tricks. He is amazing!

I asked him how he makes it look so easy.

The other kids in the team are all really nice and very good players. At training we do a lot of dribbling with the ball, three-on-three games and sometimes we get to take penalty kicks at the end. Rueben doesn't let any of the kids go home until they take a successful penalty. We all take turns being the goalkeeper and by the end of the training, all the kids and the parents are laughing their heads off because most of us are pretty hopeless at it.

We always leave the park around 6.30 p.m. and Dad does a quick trip to 7-Eleven for my Slurpee treat that I have every single week. Sometimes it is so hot that Dad has to put the car air-conditioning on full blast in my face just to cool me down. Later in the season, it is totally different, and we have to train in long pants and jackets when it is wintry and dark.

I'd prefer to play in the winter. It is way too hot in Australia for football in the summertime.

The first game I ever played was very embarrassing. When I got my first chance to kick the ball I tried too hard and my boot flew off and went further than the ball. Dad made sure that he always tied up my boots after that.

What I liked most about the first season I played was that Mum and Dad never talked about the score after the game. They only talked about the kicks, the goals, the tumbles some of the kids took and how great the team was getting. I always like it when adults are positive, just like our teachers at school. I hate it when people yell at me because I'm not doing something right. It just makes me upset.

Mrs Phillips runs the canteen at the ground and after every game, Mum buys me a big, fat bacon-and-egg roll to eat while the parents stand around and chat. Normally I drip heaps of it down the front of my shirt and on the back seat of the car. I use the tissues near the back window to clean it up without Mum and Dad noticing.

I've been playing for two years now and we usually score more goals than the teams we play against. When we start to play really competitively I think we will be hard to beat. Rueben likes the way I stay close to the back on the left side and make sure that we defend when the other team has the ball.

I'm trying to get better in my position, although sometimes you end up all over the place in games and forget exactly where you are. I haven't been able to watch too much of Steph Catley lately as she is now over in England playing for Arsenal. Dad told me that Chelsea fans don't get on too well with Arsenal fans but I don't care, she will always be my favourite, no matter what.

I can't wait to see the Matildas at the World Cup in Australia and I hope they win the gold medal. Some of the girls in the team are so famous and rich. Everybody knows who Sam Kerr is and she scores goals in every match.

What I love about football is the fun I have and the friends I make. But the thing I love most is when Mum and Dad see me kick.

CHARLIE, AGE 64

If you grew up in Western Australia during the 1960s, Australian Rules football was a staple in your sporting diet.

I have a vivid memory of my first day at Geraldton Public School: wearing ill-fitting shorts and spending the entire afternoon attempting to hide the fact that my grasp of the English language was worse than poor.

In retrospect, it is fairly clear now that my teacher was more than aware of what she was to deal with for the entire year, knowing full well that me and the other Indigenous children were destined to struggle with the basics for some time to come.

Appointed to a new post, that pretty young woman became something of a mentor to many of us. She was funny, bright, calm and loving, whilst also frustrated at much of the dysfunction she saw around her in the broader community. Australia's reluctance to truly understand and embrace Indigenous culture was and is destined to continue to produce poor educational outcomes for Aboriginal kids.

At recess on that very first day, after a morning of setting up chairs and desks and claiming a bag space on the wall directly outside the classroom, we ventured out onto the school's sports field. After an extended dry summer, it was firm, dusty and abrasive, attributes not conducive to the rough and tumble of Australian Rules football.

I'd played the game from my earliest memories, whilst three of my uncles had ventured to the Big Smoke and achieved success at lower league level in Melbourne. They were the driving forces behind my interest in the game and sport in general.

Aussie Rules presents the opportunities for freedom and expression that ignite a fire in young children, a chance to run, bounce, kick and chase in wide-open spaces. In many senses, the game is an extension of play, a fact that potentially provides the fundamental kernels of interest that capture hundreds of thousands of kids around the country every year.

In the early 1960s, the game was marked as compulsory for my class, whenever we ventured out into the Western Australian sunshine. It was the vehicle to shake off all the stresses and pent-up frustration of a few hours grappling with mathematics, grammar and spelling, things of which their mastery, to this very day, I must concede is well beyond my reach.

The Western Australian Football League was our local sports intake, with dribs and drabs of news filtering in from the South Australian equivalent and slightly more consistent content available on the powerful Victorian Football League.

Those competitions were the desired and dream destinations for many of the older boys at school who threw themselves desperately around the field, often inaccurately imitating contemporary players of which they had most likely only seen still shots in newspapers or for a few brief seconds on television.

Such is the vivid and creative mind of young children when it comes to sport, its heroes, and the sheer excitement and interest it evokes in them.

Whilst a bit of the above was evident in me, and in ad-hoc Aussie Rules play I had shown the odd bit of talent, a raw passion for it was absent. My sporting mind was to be inspired elsewhere, in a game I knew little of yet fell instantly in love with.

Somewhere near the end of my first year at primary school, as I wandered aimlessly from the toilet block back to a group of students with whom I had been sitting, I came across a boy a few years older than me.

He had a black-and-white tattered soccer ball (as everybody called it then) that looked as though it had been the only one used throughout an entire season of competitive play and he thumped it furiously into the dark brickwork at the base of the amenities wall.

He gave the ball an almighty crack and, for some unbeknownst reason to me, I wanted to do the same.

I recognised the boy as the youngest of a family of six that lived near the school with their mother. Their dad had died just a year earlier, the demon drink destroying yet another lost and displaced Indigenous family constantly battling for acceptance, opportunity and a sense of belonging.

"Whatcha doing?" I asked cautiously.

He never even looked up, continuing to pound the ball against the wall with his right foot. The sweat beads dripped steadily onto his school shirt and a small grunt emanated each and every time he put his foot through the ball.

"Can ya do any tricks?" I pressed.

Without verbally acknowledging my question he flipped the ball up with his toes and began the most perfect sequence of what I was soon to discover are called kick-ups. He kept the sphere under precise control with his right foot and then, impressively, began using each foot alternatively.

By the time he began incorporating the use of his knees and shoulders I had become completely transfixed. When he knocked the ball high into the air using his head before cushioning it with his foot once again, I felt in the presence of some sort of genius circus performer.

Curiously motivated I blurted out, "Can you teach me that?"

The boy rolled the ball towards my feet at a slow pace and when it arrived, I assumed what would become such a familiar and life-changing position: my foot on the ball and my eyes zeroed in on the target.

My first few efforts were embarrassing and met with nothing more than the odd "No", "Nup" or "Grr" from a boy desperately keen to return to his solo play. I did the best I could, kept the ball up for three consecutive kicks in a glorious moment and then reluctantly returned it to him.

I'd kicked an oval-shaped ball ever since first being handed one, swum in the local billabong from my earliest years, and run and chased with cousins and kids on a daily basis, yet nothing had ever made me feel so captivated by the challenge of controlling that ball with my feet.

I watched the boy from afar after returning to my friends, unable to take my eyes away from his endeavours for more than a second or two and the focused isolation in which he was operating.

When I arrived home that afternoon, I set about finding a way to emulate the activity as best I could. Without a spherical ball, it was to prove difficult. A split Aussie Rules ball with the bladder protruding was my starting point and was an endeavour that lasted less than five minutes.

A scuffed golf ball that had sat alongside the front steps of my family home for as long as I could remember came next and lasted no longer, with every second or third kick making a rather disturbing and crisp, cracking sound whenever the dimpled ball came in direct contact with one of the bones in my right foot.

Rather cleverly, I thought, a balloon found in the laundry cupboard became the next phase of my experiment. Filled with water, it looked the part. Needless to say, it lasted no more than one kick and made an unfortunate splat when it first left my control and landed on the gravel drive.

Never beaten, I experimented with some lightweight stones to some success and found even more with the largest acorns from the Californian oak that sat adjacent to the drive. They were far too small, yet a few of the larger ones at least provided a pain-free and engrossing challenge for a boy freshly infected with the football bug.

Knowing what I now do, a collection of leaves and rags stuffed inside an old pillow case might perhaps have been the best course of action. My mother was a skilled seamstress out of necessity and the materials to create such a thing were probably within my reach, yet my mind was not sufficiently clever to master the task.

Thus became the drill each and every afternoon. Hours of endless acorn kick-ups, with an increasing level of success and curious looks from neighbours and passers-by. I'm not sure they knew what in the world I was doing, nor did I care.

Each and every night, my final thought before sleep was how I could acquire a ball of my own.

Financially, it was an absurd suggestion to even raise with my mother. Even if it wasn't, the local stores stocked nothing more than the odd cricket bat, oval ball or tennis racquet, and a young Indigenous boy lurking around searching for anything else was far from a smart move considering the attitudes of many of the shop owners.

I kept up my practice.

Every Friday afternoon, two students in my class were asked to take the bins that held accumulated paper scraps, broken pencils and chalk fragments too small to use and dispose of the contents in the larger bins along the western fence line of the school. It was a rare thrill and the chance to wander slowly along the 100-metre track, wasting as many seconds as possible.

It took weeks to be chosen and I was thrilled when I was at last asked, buddied up with a tall Indigenous boy named Kevin to complete the mission. The metal bins were heavy and we both struggled under the weight of them. Within 20 metres of our expedition beginning, another factor became a clear challenge.

A forceful and cool afternoon breeze had sprung up and paper began jettisoning itself freely from the bins, scampering away like tumbleweeds across the landscape. Fitting the idiots we were, a chase became an attractive challenge and, without covering the rubbish that remained teetering close to the top of the bins, we left them uncovered and sprinted away after the escapees.

It didn't take too long to gather them all up. I headed north and Kevin went south, spreading ourselves across the property and snatching the loose papers with both hands as we went.

With just a couple left to snag, I stomped on one to prevent it moving in the increasing wind and saw the final target just metres ahead. Next to it was something else. Something magical.

The paper had come to rest within inches of a round leather football. It was old, worn and destined never to be found in an area of the school property where grass had been permitted to grow wildly, in an apparent effort to avoid the entire place appearing as some sort of dust bowl.

Its colour could best be described as dirt brown; there were no markings and its life story would most likely have filled a lengthy volume.

I peered towards Kevin in the distance. He was heading back to the bins with both arms full and hopelessly observing more and more paper spewing out from his grasp. Standing perhaps 20 metres from the property line, I wondered how the ball had come to rest in its current spot.

It was possibly an overzealous kick from a neighbouring property and an inability of the culprit to locate the ball soon after. Alternatively, it was perhaps a school supply of years prior or potentially just one of life's little unexplained mysteries.

For a six-year-old boy spending each and every afternoon kicking acorns around a driveway, it was nothing short of a gift from the heavens and one that was coming home by hook or by crook.

I'm proud to say that I resisted the temptation to pick up the ball and run back to Kevin and the bins screaming like a fool. The thought immediately crossed my mind that should I return to the classroom with it, confiscation could well be on the cards. Instead, I returned to assist a now very flustered classmate, who had managed to do the lion's share of the work and reclaimed the loose debris.

"What were you doing down there, Charlie? I've been working my arse off while you were staring at the grass." His voice was forceful.

Without flinching, I told my most impressive and important lie to date.

"Gwardar, froze me in my tracks."

Using the western brown snake as reasoning not only excused my extended pause on the rubbish hunt, it also prevented Kevin from venturing into that area for some time.

Before either of us could speak, the sight of our teacher standing at the top of the hill and the sound of the afternoon school bell had us bustling to the fence line to empty the bins. Potential world records were broken during the performance, as we sprinted the entire way back and hurled the bins into the corner where they resided in the classroom.

We then snatched our bags, said good afternoon to our teacher and sped towards the school gates.

I went no further than 50 metres before sitting on the roadside under a shady gum. I waited and watched as some children were collected by their parents while other kids skipped, ran and strolled in all directions towards home, as the teachers retreated to their classrooms to make preparations for the following week.

All fell silent, bar the local birds providing the stunning soundtrack to a typical Australian afternoon. I climbed the low wire school fence, ran quickly along the northern property line, cut across to the western fence and soon found the treasure.

I picked up the ball, retraced the journey, scooped up my school bag and headed home with the warmest feeling in my soul.

Walking intently, I muttered to no one in particular, "Thank you."

The next thing to overcome was the not-so-small issue of a flat football.

In another example of worldly awareness, I detoured past Sewell's Service Station, confident that should Norm the proprietor be there, he would be pleased to help me out.

Norm was one of the few white fellas I trusted. When my old man had gotten up and walked some years back, he had helped Mum out with a few second-hand pens and pencils for school and installed an old Hills Hoist for us that he had acquired from a customer who owed him a few bob.

Thankfully, he was standing in the driveway of the service station, bum up and head down under the bonnet of an obviously ill car.

"Hi, Norm. It's Charlie."

He raised his head and spun around quickly. "Hey, lad, how are ya?" he asked. His East London accent was still obvious despite 15 years in Australia.

"Good. Do ya reckon ya could pump up my ball?" I tossed the crumpled sphere to Norm and his eyebrows raised immediately.

"Wow, this is a beauty, lad. Just like the balls we used to use back in London." He rolled it around in his hands. After a moment, he took a few steps towards the fitted pump by the drive and inserted the needle into the ball. Only then did it occur to me that the bladder inside may actually be pierced and this incredible find might be destined to be more of a disappointment than a joy.

The ball inflated slowly, the anticipation inside growing with every second.

Norm unattached the pump and gave the ball a squeeze. "There ya go, lad, good as new." He bounced the ball a couple of times and then dropped it to his feet before beginning a kick-up routine very similar to the boy at school who had first triggered my love for football.

My eyes widened. "Did you play football, Norm?"

"Everyone in England plays football, lad. All day, every day." Norm kicked the ball up into his own hands, handed it to me and sent me on my way.

I resisted the temptation to attempt anything with it myself until I made it home, knowing that sending my new ball across the road into the path of an oncoming car was not a great way to start what could be the most beautiful of relationships.

The trip home took less time than usual and after launching my school bag onto the front steps and swallowing a gulp of water directly from the tap by the letter box, I kicked my new football for the first time.

I struggled, yet persisted with a clumsy kick-up routine and within 30 minutes had it under some sort of control.

That level of control was to grow in the weeks and months that followed, paralleled in growth by my mother's incessant questions about what in the world I found entertaining about kicking a ball by myself.

In reality, I think that was in fact the true attraction. The isolation in which a footballer learns the basics of their craft is compelling and intriguing; the endless quest to 'control' the ball drives the early years of the most and least talented players.

Kick-ups became easy and eventually driving the ball against the side of the house and controlling its return path ceased to be a sufficient challenge. My football development required a new trigger and it arrived in the form of a gift from the nicest white fella I ever met, Norm Sewell.

One Monday morning, my mother found a package placed neatly adjacent to the front door. It was a book, with a small note wedged inside the dust jacket that simply read, "Good luck with your football, lad. Norm."

The text was entitled *Football Made Easy* and was written by former Scottish international defender George Young. What lay inside captivated me, despite much of the language proving tough to decipher and interpret at the time.

It was filled with photos and instructional diagrams that brought the game to life in a new way. In retrospect, it is clear that the book encouraged me to think about football beyond the isolation of skill development and discover the challenge of using those skills in order to combat an opponent.

Sadly, there were no opponents for me to conquer at that time. An absence of organised play in my neck of the woods and a family income incapable of sustaining the use of an automobile that could potentially have allowed me to travel and play the game elsewhere made it impossible to participate.

I would, once again, have to improvise.

The fallen branches of gum trees twined together with porcupine grass formed a unique goal frame. An afternoon of digging saw the entire thing rooted three feet deep in the firm, dry ground and light cotton off-cuts were tied together to form the most rudimentary of nets.

Objects became opposition players, a mixture of tree stumps, branches and two old car tyres made up an outfield team of ten, whilst a large branch was deeply rooted in the centre of the goal as my goalkeeper.

The crack outfit was dribbled around, passed through and brushed off the ball as my skills improved and each and every attacking wave ended with an emphatic strike on goal and an appropriate celebration. Weekends saw this routine played out from sun up to sun down. Those early experiences still come to mind when I reflect on what football means to me as an older man and the youthful enjoyment that initially drew me to it.

By 13, a certain skill level had been achieved, admittedly against stationary opponents. However, in the end, I did find someone to play for and against.

Inspired by that chance meeting with a school student and Norm's encouragement, I headed to the Big Smoke of Perth at 15, with a dream to play competitive football and a desperate need for work. Hopping uncertainly from job to job as a young Indigenous boy, always the first to feel the effects of management's need to cut staff and maximise profits, was made somewhat easier by my involvement in the game.

It also bore a newfound and surprising awareness of just how non-racist some white fellas could be.

Playing football at a burgeoning Perth football club, experiencing feelings of belonging and community for the very first time and enjoying the game with a group of men destined to become lifelong friends all played pivotal roles in defining both my football and life journeys.

A couple of perfect kids, one supportive spouse and a whole host of challenges that occurred along the way all came to pass amidst regular Wednesday night football trainings and a liberating match awaiting on Saturday afternoons.

I'm not sure family and football life could have survived without the other. The stresses and difficulties of domesticity are diametrically opposed to the freedoms of football, yet both are so important and sustaining.

In the end, I guess my career left much to be desired in terms of competitive success. There were to be no representative honours, very few goals, a single grand final appearance, and a sore and sorry body when the boots were finally hung up at the age of 52.

However, in the most satisfying of ways, my life in football sustained me, shaped me, moulded me and calmed me. From the day I first bumped into a strange boy at school, to the act of kindness from a local white fella and all the way to the beers I drank with teammates after our final game in the over-50s, the game has given me joy.

I kept that ball too. It sits on a shelf in my office and reminds me of opportunity, something still not afforded many First Nations People and those for whom we continue our fight for cultural justice.

Perhaps if everyone had the chance to experience the discovery of such a beautiful thing and feel so blessed and fortunate to have done so, the attitudes of those born and bestowed with endless opportunity would be different.

The simplistic and humbling nature of the sphere is perhaps the greatest metaphorical leveller that exists. With just a body and ball in the contest, we are all equal.

Football germinated that awareness in me and perhaps more Australians would benefit from finding a similar vehicle to transport them to a place of greater understanding, empathy and community.

I'm very lucky that an abandoned flat football was my vehicle. Without it, I'm not sure exactly where I would be.

ISABELLA,
AGE 17

When Mum first dragged me to a netball court as the new member of a team filled with girls I barely knew, I wanted to kill her.

We have a great relationship, Mum and me. She is more like an older sister, even though I actually have Gemma to do that job. Mum is the person I head to when I need advice or a problem begins to stress me out.

I can't even remember what happened on that first day at the courts, whether we won or lost, or how well I played after just a couple of training sessions. However, there are two things that I do remember quite clearly. Firstly, how absolutely hopeless the rest of the girls in my team were, especially considering how they all talked a big game after a few seasons' experience. Secondly, I remember lying on my bed and crying when I got home.

I hated it. I still hate it.

Netball is a game played in four quarters. Each is ten minutes long and officiated by two usually very young, keen and over-zealous umpires.

More often than not, those officials are junior players eager to support their association and/or club. They are energetic young people. Obsessed with applying the rules in the most annoying way, blowing their whistle every single chance they get.

I was seven at the time of my first netball experience and with 33 courts at the park, the sound that emanated was frightful. With two umpires allocated to each court, they made the most piercing and offensive racket, with their 66 whistles blown each and every time a player stepped with the ball, contacted an opponent, ventured off-side, scored a goal or did one of apparently a million other things that only the umpires appeared to know were illegal.

The squawking and cackling of mums living vicariously through their little girls made me sick, with my mum a lot less full-on than some of the other nut-jobs watching our games. Along with many netball illiterate fathers who often became far too serious and emotionally connected to the matches, it created an overly tense and hyped mood that all of the girls hated but most never had the guts to express. It was an atmosphere that brought me to tears.

Afterwards, Mum cuddled me. She explained that it was just a bit of a shock and somehow tricked me into turning up the following weekend. She's a sneaky one, my mum.

Sadly for me, I was a very good netball player and it didn't take long to be noticed. My secret lay in natural hand-eye coordination, running speed and a burning desire to win at whatever I did. I was born with that. Mum and Gemma are a bit the same; it probably came with the DNA.

If you want to see me angry, just win against me at something. I'll churn that defeat around in my stomach and head for hours afterwards and be determined to beat you in the most comprehensive manner the next time we meet.

I can clearly remember having no real idea what I was actually doing on a netball court in the first few weeks and becoming increasingly frustrated at some of the other girls who appeared to be so apathetic towards winning and losing. That's something that to this day still drives me nuts.

I was taller, faster and able to catch and pass a ball more effectively than all of them, yet I had absolutely no idea what we were attempting to achieve. They threw the ball to me, parents screamed and I tossed it through a silly little goal.

Just seemed like a waste of time to me and I would have much rather been somewhere else.

Obviously, that was the main objective of the game, yet I was baffled as to why. It all seemed so pointless. That feeling was only multiplied when mums jumped up and down and danced with glee when I scored a goal, shouting out my name and telling me I was a champion.

I wondered if many of those mums on the sideline had ever even attempted to shoot a netball through a hoop. If they had ever tried and subsequently realised that it was not really the most challenging or important thing in the world, they perhaps may have backed off a little when it came to carrying on like a pack of squawking cockatoos.

Frankly, I would have preferred to be at home. I felt more like a guinea pig than a champion.

WHEN MUM AND DAD SEE ME KICK

We won a few that year, lost a few as well. Apparently, the other parents were all in praise of my first season. In retrospect, I should have been playing in a much more competitive and enthusiastic team, or perhaps a different sport altogether.

I played a couple of seasons of netball for a different club, after insisting to Mum that the current mob were an utter waste of time. I was probably too young to be able to really express just how unfulfilling I found the game and how I desperately wanted to be involved in something a little more physical and less structured.

Any sport that requires players to stop when they have the ball seems pretty silly to me.

Watching my older brother enjoying that sort of freedom made me jealous. Being dragged along to rugby league matches each Sunday fuelled that jealousy. The wild aggression in the game excited me, as opposed to running around a court wearing a silly little bib and playing some sort of restrictive game of musical chairs, where all the competitors had to cease movement and freeze each and every time the whistle was blown.

The rugby league coach would roar at his players, boys would take heavy hits and lie motionless on the ground, and slightly unhinged parents would tread very close to the line when it came to offering advice to the referees in control of the contest.

Whilst there was something a little uneasy about the game, its rawness, bravery and aggression had me keen to play it, or something else that evoked the same feelings.

My brother Oliver is a piece of work. With just one training session and an organised game to play each week, there were plenty of hours for him to practise at home. Who better to play the opposition than his little sister? That extended well beyond the backyard and the odd kick, tackle or chase. Opposition we became in more ways than one, as Oliver took on the mission of teasing and tormenting in true big-brother style.

On many occasions, I ended up throwing an object at him or calling him every name under the sun, before eventually earning a cuddle from Mum. Oliver chuckled away quietly in his bedroom after being sent there to reflect on his behaviour.

My brother pushed me, poked me, tripped me, bashed me, tickled me, teased me and, most importantly, toughened me up. That toughness was an attribute that would serve me well when Mum finally got the message and went hunting for other sports for me to play.

Oztag was a cinch with my speed. In fact, the guy who wrote the book you are reading coached me in my very first season. He stood on the sideline and yelled and screamed much like the mums at netball. We learnt the basics despite rarely winning a game.

I scored most of the team's tries off the back of actually being able to hold on to the ball and run. Neither are the most amazing of skills really, yet considering the poor standard of the opposition we were up against, I looked like a star. Even though I was actually far from it.

Touch football was pretty much the same and very few girls could keep up with me in school athletics events. The fact that I was prepared to have a crack at pretty much anything spoke volumes about not being able to find a sport that interested me. No matter the activity, the level of satisfaction was never deep. Any enjoyment usually stemmed from interaction with other competitors and the cheap and temporary satisfaction that comes with earning a trophy or two.

As an athlete I was craving something far more satisfying, but when I began playing football at age nine, everything changed.

Castle Hill United was my first football club. Founded in 1972, it has become one of the largest in the Hills Football Association in the North West of Sydney. Mum was really proud of my decision to play for them. She was born and bred in the area and we still live close to where she had caused a heck of a lot of trouble as a teenager about 30 years ago. Sorry, Mum.

It is hard to explain exactly what it was that initially excited me so much about the game. Expressing the feelings I had at those early training sessions is difficult. It just seemed so free, so open, and more primal and exciting than running around a netball court with an annoying umpire blowing their whistle in my face every 25 seconds.

I fell in love with football very, very quickly.

A few seasons with Castle Hill taught me a lot. We were well coached and my role as a defender was established fairly early on. Despite still learning the basics of the game, my strategy in defence was a simple one; I would use my superior speed to sweep across the defensive area and tidy up a host of problems that the bad defending of others had caused.

WHEN MUM AND DAD SEE ME KICK

After doing so, I'd have a bit of a run through the midfield and play the ball forward for one of our more attacking players to pick up and hopefully find the back of the net. It worked most of the time, yet my role changed somewhat when we came up against a superior team that constantly threatened our goal.

That meant a tough day. Mentally, I felt the need to cover every player and every angle, not confident that teammates would be able to repel the attacks and stop goals being scored.

Mum copped a bit of flak for the way I played, with some of the other parents feeling that my attempt to dominate the game was somehow an insult to their child. In reality, I just hated seeing the ball go in the back of our net. It made me feel sick. It still does.

I would have done anything to stop the opposition scoring and knew for certain that many of the other kids I played with did not share the same passion for doing so. Therefore, I was determined to help them and do a portion of their job if the game required it. Not for them, but for me.

I was the one who would replay the key moments of the game in my head over the next 24 hours, furious that I could potentially have done better in the same circumstances. I knew the other players would be off to barbeques, parties and activities that afternoon, oblivious to the mistakes they had made, the goals they'd conceded and the impact that had had on the overall result.

Of course it sounds selfish, yet we are all hard-wired in different ways and I wanted to win.

By the time I was 12, height had become something of an asset to me. I'm no giant, but I'm taller than average and when that fortunate attribute was combined with my natural speed and somewhat controversial aggression, Mum was approached by some interested clubs in Sydney that expressed hopes of having me join their teams.

It was all a little strange really. I felt like the slightly over-aggressive defender that other clubs were scouting for my size, abnormal will to win and toughness, rather than being actually able to play football well.

I had watched Alanna Kennedy, Clare Polkinghorne and Steph Catley for the Matildas and seen exactly the same qualities, as well as a ruthlessness in defending that is a not-negotiable when it comes to achieving success. I decided that I would more than happily be described as playing football in the same way. I was pretty sure Alanna, Clare and Steph knew exactly what they are doing.

After some toing and froing, Mum and I settled on joining a National Premier League 2 club in Sydney for the 2020 season, where I would take my next steps in a football journey that was becoming increasingly satisfying.

Playing in the women's second tier, the club was not a successful one at the underage level, yet it was developing and potentially a nice place to start at age 14.

Any thoughts of my introduction to the club providing an instant boost in results were laid to rest very quickly, with some of the dominant teams in the league putting goals past us with ease throughout my first season.

The same feelings of frustration were there, as girls mistimed kicks, failed to track back with opposition players, and felt reluctant to enter challenges with the force required to either win the ball or kill the attacking movement.

For much of that first season, I played in relative silence, not quite confident enough to take on a leadership role, one where pointing out the mistakes and poor efforts that were costing us so dearly on the pitch would be allowed and listened to. That led to countless sleepless nights and many long, reflective and quiet drives home from far-flung football pitches across New South Wales.

As any footballer knows, a losing team can become a dysfunctional and tense environment. That appeared to be where things were headed as my first season of NPL play concluded and the competition took its usual Christmas recess.

Despite fears of returning after what had been an unsuccessful debut season, another year in the centre of defence loomed and that positional reality brought about one of the biggest challenges of all.

Alongside me in the back four was a girl with whom I never saw eye to eye. I thought she was whiny and soft, not a player anything like the kind of warrior I wanted to play alongside. The relationship between us was not particularly good to start, soured the more we lost and eventually became a blame game where we both handled ourselves in a less-than-classy way.

If a cleverly weighted ball was ever threaded through the centre of defence and a goal resulted, our eyes would meet, both sets clearly of the view that blame lay with the other and that this was not the first time it had happened. It was somewhat childish in a way, yet we were still children. No doubt some of the greatest centre-back pairings in football history have had similar tensions and hot spots in their relationships.

The problem for both of us was that the coach was unable to calm the waters, seemingly beginning to take the side of my defensive partner. Parents of a few other players also appeared to be united in their concerns over my attitude and aggression.

Looking back, I feel awful about the whole situation.

Aurelia is a really nice girl and someone I now call a friend. Maybe our egos drove us apart as we both strived to become the best players we could be and perhaps that is a normal thing within a football team that isn't winning. It may have been mostly my fault or perhaps we should both share some of the blame.

It doesn't really matter now. What does is that we are both developing well as footballers. In fact, Aurelia is killing it and playing at the top level of NPL football in New South Wales. Who knows, we may even find ourselves together in a defensive back four at some stage. I reckon we would be pretty hard to stop.

At the time, though, team spirit continued to erode as results worsened and the idea of playing football elsewhere became a very attractive proposition when Mum first raised it. Players were leaving the pitch and reporting their frustrations to teammates and parents on a weekly basis. Mums and dads were seeing little development in their daughters' skill sets and the club's technical director insisted we persist with a formation and style of play that appeared destined to produce nothing but loss after loss.

Thanks to a tip-off Mum received from a friend, the opportunity to trial with the Fleetwood Town International Academy's Australian hub arose in early 2021, with the hunt for a new club well underway at the same time.

The hub is run by a man named James Boyle and its intention is to identify talented Australian players and potentially see them venture to England to play, study and train at the academy base in Thornton-Cleveleys.

Currently, the players at the academy are male and come from all over the world. It includes boys from North America, Africa, Asia and Australia, but sadly, no females as yet. With the rise of women's football continuing, it is difficult to imagine that 'boys only' situation remaining a reality for too much longer.

I must admit to having a bit of trouble understanding what James says now and then. He has a Scottish accent that reminds me a little of Mike Myers' character Fat Bastard from the film *Austin Powers: The Spy Who Shagged Me*.

We first met on a humid summer afternoon, where we had arranged a one-on-one trial. After a brief chat, James put me through the toughest set of skill and fitness drills I had ever experienced. Apparently, he told Mum immediately after the session that I was in, so impressed he was. If only he knew just how confused, flustered and out of breath I had felt whilst completing the session.

Whatever I had done, it appeared to have impressed him and I couldn't help but think that the hard and sustained session, featuring nothing even like a moment of relief, was exactly what I should have been doing for the last few years.

As a new season approached, I was now a member of the Australian hub of the Fleetwood Town Academy, yet strangely was no longer connected to a club. That situation needed a resolution in quick time and as Mum and I searched for the perfect fit, James pushed me hard and threw me in with the academy boys.

Talk about a red rag to a bull. The idea of competing physically with players as committed and passionate about the game as I was brought out an even greater level of hunger and competitiveness.

After pounding our bodies through a rigid set of fitness drills, James would set up grids, cones and equipment to create a circuit of skill-based drills that required immense concentration and physical strength to complete.

There was sprinting, lateral movement, heading, jumping, ball control, passing and balance-promoting drills in every session. Within weeks I was fitter, faster and stronger, as well as more confident than I had ever been.

However, that confidence was to be tested after a phone call from a new club came, asking me to attend their trials for the upcoming season. After a diligent process of investigation, the club appeared to be an ideal location for me. It was a fairly new club with big plans for their women's program.

Mum likes to say that I interviewed the coach rather than the other way around and I did ask every question imaginable when we spoke on the phone. The style we intended to play, the experience of the other players, leadership roles and realistic expectations for the season were all discussed and at the completion of the conversation, a confidence had been built that the club might indeed be the best fit for me.

However, as if to emphasise the difference between appearance and reality, something felt a little off from the moment I arrived.

The players around me seemed a little light on for size and enthusiasm. The verbal message emanating from the coach sounded a little unsure and inconsistent and as soon as the first session began I could sense that the approach to the training being undertaken was nowhere near the level that James sought to achieve.

There was no formal warm-up procedure, no warm-down after the session and when I asked the reason as to why, the coach simply replied, "I don't believe in it."

I left the training pitch in tears—not something of which I am not proud, yet the thought of missing an entire season of football sent a fear through me that brought the most awful of uncertainties.

As usual, Mum was there and just as we planned to strategise our next move, opportunity knocked.

By the time we arrived home from the trial, news of my rather unflattering departure had reached another NPL club. They were apparently interested in taking a punt on an unproven yet extremely keen player. Despite carrying a lingering and troublesome ankle injury that required regular physiotherapy, the chance to redeem myself in person in the days that followed was simply too good to refuse.

Nepean Football Club was to be my new home, a club begun as recently as 2010 and one built to cater for the ever-growing population of Western Sydney.

The players sized me up pretty quickly in the early sessions, keen to see whether the new girl had anything to add to what was already a decent team. I copped a few hard challenges and could sense that there were a few defenders keen to show me their best.

It was far from easy and the training I had done with James held me in good stead. Without it, I may have been struggling. Each and every on-the-ball contest was physical, no player appeared held above any other and reputations meant little when it came to a contested ball; you either won it or lost it and then prepared yourself for the next one, keen to do better.

The feeling of a clean slate was refreshing and the emotional comfort felt led to an openness and almost instant relationships and camaraderie. I had played in good teams, fun teams, bad teams and dysfunctional teams, yet knew a happy team the moment I saw one.

Sadly, our 2022 season did not play out as we had hoped. Along with many others, I suffered an injury, girls were dropping like flies with COVID-19 through the cold of winter and plenty of games had to be postponed.

We were nearer the bottom of the ladder than the top and I twice missed the chance to go toe to toe with Aurelia and my old club, once when forced onto the bench with a broken arm early in the season. Being able to work on fitness with James whilst recovering was a bonus and a few wins did come late in the year, yet we were well off the pace as a team, something that never feels nice.

Nepean has a feeder arrangement with the Western Sydney Wanderers A-League Women's team and I would be lying if I said that the thought of playing top class football in Australia hasn't crossed my mind.

Whether I even have a chance of achieving that is something I think about often, wondering how much more improvement would be required to get there.

Many young girls are dreaming of the Matildas, yet the reality of how good a player needs to be to make it to that level reminds me of just how much work they have done to get there. Sometimes I wonder whether I am prepared to do that work, especially every time my ankle swells up or fatigue sets in.

Adults always tell me that playing football is a journey involving both the fun of playing the game and the development of friendships and relationships that can last a lifetime. At the moment, it is all about playing for me.

I am not too sure exactly where my football journey will take me or just how successful it will be, but hopefully I can play at senior NPL 1 level in the years to come and become a respected enough defender for A-League clubs to take a look at and consider. That is my dream, but there is a lot of training, development and dedication ahead before that might happen.

School and work commitments do make it tough at times, yet Mum's always around for advice and as long as she avoids netball courts on the long drives to football pitches on Sundays, I'll be happy.

ALI,
AGE 48

If anyone ever wants to talk about what life is like for a refugee in Australia, I'd be happy to chat. As a seven-year-old boy, my family and I arrived in Sydney via boat and set about forging a new life in what we instantly thought of as the most beautiful country we had ever seen.

My father was an abusive man, often drunk, violent and uncompromising. My mother suffered daily, desperately trying to instil some sense of normality into the family unit. Her efforts were relatively successful and my sister Samira and I enjoyed enough of our upbringing to say quite convincingly that it was well short of an utter disaster.

Despite the tense and foreboding atmosphere that existed on a daily basis in and around the family home, we emotionally forgave our father.

Hassan was a proud Palestinian man, one determined to return to the family home that had been overtaken by Israeli soldiers in the summer of 1949. Like thousands of others, his father had held on to the keys to their home, in the hope of one day returning. Yet over time, as the occupation extended and the new developments which were housing Israeli settlers increased, the chances of ever getting home diminished.

As rebellion and resistance became the norm among many in the Palestinian community, the suspicion of Israeli forces grew. Nightly, they would raid homes, intimidate families and take away anyone involved or suspected of colluding with rebel groups.

It led to a reign of terror and fear that continues to this day.

As police and military vehicles streamed down the dusty streets, mothers hid their teenage sons for fear of their potential detention. They were the prime targets of the Israelis, who knew full well that an insurgence against the state was destined to be borne among the angry, politically aware and idealistic youth who still held hopes of a return to a Palestinian state. It was a hope that many of their elders had already cast aside.

Hassan told stories of the relative poverty in which he and his family lived. They had been paid a pittance to work in the olive groves they had once owned, unable to purchase anything other than the barest of essentials.

That meant basic Middle Eastern food on a nightly basis. Bread, a few simple dips prepared by his mother and, on a good day, a small portion of whatever meat had come their way via bartering or sheer luck.

One such night, a patrol of Israeli soldiers burst through the front door of the farmyard shack that had become their home. The intruders screamed violently, pushed and shoved the family back into their chairs around the table, groping Hassan's mother as they heckled and mocked her appearance.

Hassan trembled with fear and after nearly five years of displacement and a burning fury around the injustice that had seen his family crumble from a respected and influential one in the community to such a peasant-like existence, his father had simply had enough.

As Hassan watched in terror, his father stood up and firmly yet simply said to the Israeli soldiers, "Get out of my house!"

One of the men immediately raised his weapon and bluntly thrust the butt of the rifle in the direction of Hassan's father's temple. The immense blow had the desired effect and my grandfather fell to the ground instantly and lay motionless.

The soldiers spat on Hassan's mother and threatened to return and have their way with his sister. They thumped his father across the back of the head with a small lamp that sat on a table by the front door, then left.

As the soldiers departed the family went to their father's aid. His eyes were notably sunken. Amidst the screams and tears of his mother, Hassan watched in terror as her frantic attempts to revive her husband failed.

My grandfather was dead within minutes. Hassan was nine years old.

It was an experience that was to haunt the man destined to be my father and was perhaps the primary motivator behind the person he was to become over the next 50 years.

He loved my mother and us children and worked hard to try to provide the best life possible for us all. Yet he lived as a man with something else always on his mind. Something dark and explosive that in unpredictable moments would bubble to the surface.

Many years later, I saw him attack a disc jockey at a family wedding because he saw a resemblance to the man who had killed his father. On one occasion he let a real estate agent have it with both barrels after the innocent man had dared knock on our family home in Sydney and enquire whether we were thinking of selling.

"YOU WILL NOT TAKE MY HOUSE. IT IS MINE!" he bellowed at the young man, who looked like a rookie making his way in the real estate game.

I felt so sorry for him.

At least once a week there would be a significant outburst, laced with the Israeli occupation of his land and the night his own father was murdered right before his eyes.

Hassan met my mother 21 years after his father's death. He was handsome, she was beautiful. They married in 1970 and continued to live in the confusing reality of occupied life in their homeland. I was born on the concrete floor of the same house in which my grandfather was killed; my sister was born just two years later.

Rather bizarrely, amidst the yelling and tension of living in such an environment and with a man so psychologically affected by it, my childhood had plenty of happiness in it.

Perhaps it was the ignorance to the political realities that made it so, yet other local children became friends. My sister ran a hairdressing service to the community that would form the foundations of the successful business she would eventually set up in Australia. And me? I played football.

About 15 boys aged between six and 13 formed what we rather comically called Palestine United. We had no pitch on which to play, but we did have a dusty area alongside our house that was quickly lined with sticks and shaped into what we felt was something like Wembley Stadium. Not that any of us actually knew what Wembley Stadium was at the time, of course.

Goals were fashioned from tree branches and bound with vines. One of the younger boys provided a ball that he claimed had been pinched from an Israeli's backyard—this always gave us great satisfaction, although he had been known to seek out a bit of attention at times. Outside school hours, football became our life.

Initially, the skill level was awful, yet picked up briskly over the countless time and immense energy we poured into the game. Ultra-competitive matches only came to a close at sundown when mothers' voices echoed across the neighbourhood and boys were beckoned home.

I had the luxury of a few kick-ups on my home pitch before I went inside, enjoying the solace of the setting and guessing what sort of mood my father would be in when I went in to eat.

At age seven, my father announced that the family would be immigrating to Australia. It was the strangest sentence I had ever heard.

I cried for the loss of my Palestinian life, my friends and my football. I also had zero knowledge of Australia; frankly, I thought it was on the mainland of Europe.

To this day I have no idea how the arrangements were made, for how long my father had hatched the plan, nor how my mother felt about following a man with a serious mental illness to the other side of the world and trusting his decision to do so.

In January of 1977, we disembarked a large boat in Sydney. We saw the Opera House, Harbour Bridge and the stunning harbour.

As we peered across the scene on a scorching summer's day, I remember uttering to myself, "Ayn nahn bism allah?" Translated to English, it means, "Where in God's name are we?" More accurately, for an Aussie, it means, "Where the fuck am I?"

I don't remember too many specifics of those early months. It was all something of a blur as we bed-hopped from cousin's house to old friend's apartment to rancid hostel. All the while, my father was working his backside off in the background, struggling with government authorities in an attempt to gain the keys to the house for which he longed.

Eventually, he did it.

Punchbowl, a not new yet flourishing suburb in the southwest of Sydney, was to be our new home. It suited us well. The local schools were walking distance away, an important fact considering the finances to purchase a new car were still well out of my father's reach, and the nearest mosque was two suburbs away in Lakemba.

We set about building a life, realising quickly that we were surrounded by hundreds of fellow Middle-Eastern people who had also left the region. People, like us, sick to death of the constant tension and unrest that was far from conducive to raising a family.

WHEN MUM AND DAD SEE ME KICK

There were Lebanese restaurants, coffee shops, greengrocers and mixed business stores popping up all over the place. Despite the sometimes curious and judgemental eyes of the Anglo-Saxon locals, the sense of community we quickly built sustained us and were the kernels of true belonging.

My father took a job in a furniture factory on Canterbury Road, slightly west of where we lived. It changed our lives instantly. The quality of nightly dinners improved out of sight, shopping trips were planned, where Samira and I were gifted clothes that resembled the styles worn by most of the children our own age, and gradually items of furniture were purchased to fill out the modest three-bedroom home that we had been allocated by the state on a rental basis.

Of course, there was nothing lavish about any of the purchases, all done on a still strict budget, yet it was almost palatial when compared to what we had experienced in Palestine.

Memories of the night my father insisted we become real Aussies and take a trip to Punchbowl McDonald's still make me smile. I had heard all the kids at Punchbowl Boys High School talk about this Big Mac thing and was intrigued.

By then, my father had his first car, a Toyota Corona into which we had to cram, despite the fact there was only four of us. We parked at the golden arches and entered a store with long Saturday night lines, waited patiently and guessed what we might like when we made it to the counter.

I'm fairly sure my father's broken English may have led to a few unexpected items arriving on our tray. However, his request for a "Bigga Macca" definitely made it through and I devoured my first ever burger with sheer delight. On reflection, I am so pleased that my parents were not too fundamental in adhering to Islamic laws around Halal food at the time.

To this day, I never drive past that store without pulling in, buying a Big Mac and sitting quietly on my own. For a McDonald's store to hold such a sentimental place in someone's heart may seem a little strange. But to me it means everything.

Having become active members of the local community and growing in confidence as the months rolled by, my father and I took a walk to Punchbowl Park one Saturday morning. A vast expanse of playing fields was set up, tennis courts filled with matches underway and the main oval prepared for what looked an important football match, based on the number of people seated in the large grandstand.

It was a place with which I was to become familiar. In an escape that my father's moods tended to necessitate, I would sit in that stand, alone, dreaming of being on the pitch and playing the game I loved.

Harassing my father was not a smart move. Ask the question, receive the answer and walk away was the proven and best course of action, one that my sister and I had learnt and perfected over the years. Yet when it came to football, I pushed.

I wanted to play and asked my father three days in a row. Despite fearing a mighty wallop across the head each time, I persisted out of passion.

To my astonishment, in February 1978, he said quite simply, "I'll see what I can do, Ali."

I nearly wet my pants.

In truth, it wasn't that difficult to get me involved in the game at the time. There were a host of local clubs all looking for players, registration fees were far less offensive than they are today and ethnic communities of all flavours had become involved decades earlier.

Apparently, my father had asked around at the Punchbowl Hotel—he was also a little loose on the no alcohol thing, and made friends with a few of the dads whose sons played park football. Trials were in March. "Bring him down," they said. It was as easy as that.

It didn't stop my father explaining how much effort, time and money he had invested in getting me started in Australian football. I could not have cared less about the process required to get me involved. Kicking a ball was all that mattered.

My Punchbowl team seemed a perfect fit, with plenty of Lebanese boys involved and many Palestinian Australians being mistaken for and claiming to be Lebanese at the time. It was a sad part of Palestinian migration around the world that it was often easier to cite another land of birth than attempt to explain and prove to the narrow-minded that Palestine was not a home of stone-throwing terrorists.

The internal shame of not proudly proclaiming one's true heritage lies with you forever.

Football provided the outlet that a young migrant boy needed as he adjusted to a new life. I thrived. Firstly, I had many of the other boys covered for skill. Secondly, I was something of a novelty that saw a nickname labelled on me in quick time.

WHEN MUM AND DAD SEE ME KICK

I was born with the lower part of my right arm missing, just below the elbow. It never really hampered me too much. I could do everything with my left, including knock down a Big Mac with ease. With so many other, more significant challenges faced in my formative years, it was often the furthest thing from my mind.

However, it did raise a few questions at football training.

"Where's your arm, mate?" was always the bluntest of these questions. There were also more thoughtful enquiries like, "What's the stump feel like?" or "Can we have a feel?"

Whilst potentially polarising, my disability was quickly forgotten when my teammates struggled to take possession of the ball as I dribbled past them. As a fleet-footed midfielder alongside the coach's son, Craig McKewen, on the left side of attack, the season ahead looked promising.

It looked even more emotionally satisfying when the nickname arrived during a warm-up match at Punchbowl Park. As the ball dribbled over the sideline after making contact with an opponent's foot, I was the nearest player in the vicinity and required to take the quick throw.

The penny dropped for the coach and manager nearby, probably foolishly wondering why they had not thought of this situation earlier.

"It's okay, Ali, we'll get someone else to take it," said the coach, well within earshot and somewhat embarrassed for me.

I replied, "It's okay, coach, I can do it."

Using a much-rehearsed technique, I hoisted the ball above my head with my left hand before tilting my head and reaching across with my shorter limb to support the ball with both. There was a stunned silence.

It made vision a little tricky, yet years of practice had taught me to aim a little further right than others would, as the ball tended to drift to the left with my left-side dominance. I completed the throw and the ball nestled at the feet of McKewen.

He passed the ball off and shouted loudly enough for all the parents to hear. "Holy shit. It's Ali the one-armed bandit!"

These days, Craig may well be told that his comment was thoughtless, insensitive and discriminatory. However, for a Palestinian boy disguised as a Lebanese migrant playing football in a new country in 1978, it was music to my ears.

From that day on, I was known as 'the one-armed bandit'.

Each and every time I heard it expressed aloud, it was done so with admiration, affection and love. Members of opposition teams would say to me, "Oh, you're that one-armed bandit guy," and I loved every minute of it.

Our team excelled; I played a key role and felt whole. A buggered arm and the game of football had made me feel like I belonged. Relationships were forged that are as strong today as they ever were. The notion of the unifying power of a football club was never more apt than in the role the game played in offering something to me that was missing, required and set to become a fulcrum around which life revolved.

Now, I'm certain no one recognises the one-armed guy at Punchbowl McDonald's, chugging down a Big Mac at two o'clock on a Tuesday afternoon. They would have no idea that he does so in honour of his brave and now deceased mother and father, who took he and his sister there for dinner in an effort to feel part of Australian society.

Nobody there would know of his football past, nor his nickname.

But Craig McKewen would. He used it in his speech as best man at my wedding. It is still how he refers to me when we meet for Wednesday night trivia most weeks.

It is also a key component of the stories he tells my son, also named Craig, when he reminds him just how good a footballer his dad was.

JOHNNY,
AGE 56

The number of lads I have seen head-butted in pubs is astonishingly high. It would have to be at least 200.

It is probably not something of which the game nor the people involved in it should be proud, but the majority of those incidents were fuelled by football matches playing out on television screens as the grog flowed and bravado grew.

My mother always encouraged me to avoid such violence and I'm pleased to say that, for the most part, I have. Yet growing up in the East End of London meant that the chances of living a life without seeing a fair bit of male aggression play out before my very eyes was fairly slim.

Holbrook Road, West Ham E13 was my local haunt as a boy.

Like most of the lads around me, there was little to write home about when it came to the digs we occupied as families, nor the general financial struggles that lurked as a constant reminder of where we stood in the socioeconomic pecking order. Our home was shit, the old boy was drunk most of the time and my mother could be a nasty creature depending on her mood and how much of a battering she had copped from him the night prior.

Most nights I shut my eyes and wished as earnestly as I could that I was somewhere else, anywhere else.

I was an utter failure at school, a train wreck when it came to wooing the opposite sex in the years that followed, and seemingly destined for a life in mundane and repetitive factory work.

That all probably leads you to believe that this is undoubtedly going to be the saddest and most gruesome chapter in this book, but thanks to football, it isn't.

Somehow, the challenges of an underprivileged childhood were cloaked, thanks to the game that I loved to play. It is of course such a simple game, yet one that engrossed me as a boy and sustains me still.

In fact, it means a whole lot more to me now than it ever did. Time has provided a level of appreciation for and an understanding of the game that I never dreamed possible. Now as a middle-aged man, it looks like a completely different thing. It seems bigger, more meaningful and powerful. A metaphor for something so much more important.

At first it was just a physical challenge, as I hacked away at the legs of the local boys every afternoon.

All wearing our tatty black school shoes and increasingly damaging them as we played football on the rough cobbled and asphalt surfaces near our homes, we took no prisoners in our efforts to claim possession of the ball. Blood was regularly shed, emotions strained and the odd fist flung in the passionate play that thoughts of still make me smile to this day.

Some of those lads have now passed. Many I've not had contact with for decades and others I'd struggle to recognise if I crossed paths with them in the street. However, unknowingly, we were all fostering a love for the game every time we kicked a ball, each time we were pissed off at conceding and on every occasion that mums and dads dragged us by the ear, back into the house for a reluctant tea.

In those days, the game was comprehended in the most simplistic of ways. Later, whilst playing in more structured environments, coaching and placing greater importance on developing skill in younger players, the lens through which I viewed the game changed somewhat.

With a home life steadily eroding and football providing the only satisfactory distraction from a potentially cyclical life, the game kept me alive. Adopting the traits, habits and personalities of those who had shaped my understanding and view of the world was a frightful thought and as something of an escape, football helped me avoid doing it.

Somehow, there was no depression, nor a powerful enough temptation to lure me into a life of violence or crime. There was plenty of frustration and anger, yet football balanced life, enabling a young and impressionable boy to enter his teenage years without jumping aboard the dangerous and wayward bandwagon that many of my peers chose to ride.

Instead, my mind was constantly filled with images of football pitches, players and sporting poetry.

Whilst much yelling took place at home and the sound of objects bouncing off walls became more frequent the later the hour of the day, I often hid inside my built-in wardrobe. It was a rather poorly constructed and cumbersome thing and to a small boy, appeared as old as time itself. Yet it did possess a solid flat floor that was comfortable enough if a cushion or two was used to lessen the firmness of it.

Inside, I had secretly gathered an array of art and craft materials that had been pinched and borrowed, or, as I prefer to say, a collection of materials that I had procured from various places on my travels.

There were bits and pieces I'd snatched from school, justifying such behaviour by citing them as surplus supplies, other items that had been spotted in public rubbish bins and about a quarter of all the materials I had collected were found in Mrs Dobbins' bin at number 14, just three doors down from our home.

She was a school teacher who often jettisoned pens, matchsticks, glue, felt paper, as well as art and craft gold in the form of cardboard offcuts, that suited my purpose to a tee. I also had old buttons, pins, paper clips, toilet rolls and tissue paper.

At the centre of my thinking was the fact that no one was to know what I was doing. Had it been discovered, the very thing that sustained the slim hopes I had that there was indeed a better world, a better place for me, would have been snatched away. Subterfuge was required.

An old hard-backed school suitcase provided the security I needed. After each session in my cave, any unused resources were folded, closed, placed in small jars, organised in neat piles and returned to the case.

It was then closed, locked with a rather rusty and ineffective padlock I had found on the street, and placed towards the back of the wardrobe, hidden under three pairs of shoes which I had well and truly outgrown.

What I created from the materials presented a slightly more difficult proposition in terms of where they were to be hidden. Unlikely as it was that my parents would ever care enough or find the time to sniff around the space and expose my little secret, the mere thought of it scared the heck out of me. It was paramount in my thinking that should the unthinkable ever occur, the chances of them making an astonishing discovery and exposing my little workshop and its creations had to be no better than zero.

A rather ostentatious rug that covered a broken floorboard provided the perfect cover. Cracking the rotting timber further, I was able to remove a section around 12 inches long and reach comfortably into the subfloor.

There, inside a simple cardboard shoe box, I would hide my little football world. A simple relocating of the bed meant that the access point existed somewhere near the foot of it and was never to be discovered or disturbed by parents to whom the notion of cleaning thoroughly was utterly foreign.

What I made in my dark and cramped art and craft studio were little footballers. A simple flat cardboard base was topped with a paper clip, used to roughly structure the player's body. That was fleshed out with tightly scrunched coloured tissue paper, designed to match the kit of the team for whom the player represented.

A button was glued on top, a face of sorts, with glitter, cotton wool or tissue paper used as hair.

Frankly, they were not particularly convincing and, since I was blessed with limited artistic talent, their quality barely improved as time passed.

Some weeks the speed of production hummed along with four or five little footballers in the works at the same time. During others, opportunities to tuck myself away in the safe space I had carefully created were rare.

Schoolwork never hindered the hobby and poor results clearly reflected my priorities at the time. Yet absurd family drives to the homes of relatives and an afternoon of beer-swilling, bad singing and my subsequent embarrassment towards the people who modelled irresponsibility all so well always had me wishing I could have just been left behind.

Such trips ate significantly into the time available on weekends to work on my footballers and opportunities were sometimes scarce during the week. Most afternoons were spent playing the game with friends before returning inside for a nightly meal in a state of utter exhaustion.

Thus, the creation of 54 little hand-crafted football players took near three years, until I stopped at the age of 14.

Just as I have no real memory as to how the original concept came upon me in the first place, the reason for it ending also remains a mystery. A little like Forrest Gump, perhaps I just started running, reached a point in time and simply stopped.

That was May 1978.

At that time, Nottingham Forest had its hands clasped around silverware, winning the title race for the English Division One Championship by seven points. Liverpool had chased them home, with Everton, Manchester City and Arsenal making up the remainder of the top five.

Sadly, Leicester City and Newcastle United won just 11 games between them to assure themselves of relegation. My heart was broken when West Ham lost 2–0 to Liverpool on the final day to also condemn themselves to the Second Division for the following season. Perhaps that awful and hollow feeling of relegation played a role in my demotivation, or maybe the boy was just getting a little too old to be hiding away in a wardrobe, dreaming of escape and crafting caricatures of football players.

Whichever it was, the collection was transferred from the shoebox to the tattered case and destined to be locked and stowed away for what ended up being 34 years.

Inside the case lay Hammers stars Bryan Robson, David Cross and Trevor Brooking, Scottish heroes in the form of Kenny Dalglish and Andy Gray, as well as the two top scorers in that 1977/78 domestic season, Bob Latchford and Trevor Francis.

With limited access to broadcasts of international matches at the time, the collection was very English-centric, yet I had attempted three-time Ballon d'Or winner Johan Cruyff and also constructed a very poor representation of Pele, based mostly on mental images of newspaper photographs rather than any visual evidence that I possessed.

With its contents now locked away, the case containing the football dreams of a broken-hearted, lost and often sad little boy was to stay with him for the rest of his life, destined to remain a powerful reminder of things that he lacked the courage to speak of.

The expected and eventual catastrophic destruction of the family unit in West Ham occurred, somewhat macabrely, with the untimely deaths of both parents setting me free. With no academic qualifications on which to lean, the factories of London were calling. Employment was far from a given in the mid-1980s, especially for young men not suited to or qualified for a life in the professional world.

By then, West Ham United had done its time a tier down. It took three seasons, but the mighty claret and blue returned to the top flight in 1981/82.

From factory to factory I roamed, seeking financial security, community and belonging. Conditions were frequently criminal, expectations absurd and short stints of around a month or two became the norm for many young men at the time.

Flat after flat followed, with finances strained, landlords quick to pounce and often only well-meaning friends keeping a roof over my head. Life was tough, yet playing football in a formal setting for the first time was to produce a sense of exhilaration that quite simply took my breath away.

The after-school football madness as a boy had been fun, no doubt, yet when a tall Dutchman working alongside me in a London paint factory asked if I might like to join his team and play football on a Sunday, I'm not sure I realised how powerful the decision to do so would become.

1985/86 was my first ever season of competitive play and I took it all very seriously, just as West Ham United was producing its greatest ever season of English domestic football. The grind of factory life had become my norm and I was already using football as a security blanket to sustain my mental health.

I threw myself into the game with vigour and became a pretty damn good footballer in what was a keen and decently skilled league. As something of a Sunday League star, there were moments where I considered taking the game even more intently. Who knows, with any serious training and a more professional approach I may have even carved out a career in the lower English leagues.

However, in 1988, at the age of 24, and despite a little talent and an undoubted passion for the game, the realisation that success on the pitch was delivering little of what I craved led to an abrupt retirement.

I walked away feeling that I would never play again.

Looking back, the decision was made with a clear subconscious intention. Whilst pats on the back after goals and the sheer joy of kicking a ball both remained wonderful feelings, it was in fact emotional stability that I sought.

Unable to articulate such a thought at the time, it is now clear that my decision to cease playing competitively and seek friendship, a sense of community and belonging was a necessity. In reflection, it is clear that for as far back as I can remember, a void existed and life was destined to remain unfulfilled until change took place.

As is the case for most of us, important life decisions are not always executed flawlessly. Yet looking back, the choice I made appears as a well-considered and measured one and has led directly to a life filled with more joy than I ever thought possible.

It helped me find community, friendship and nurtured the ability to trust people unconditionally, something a dysfunctional working class upbringing does not encourage.

Through that period and all the other key forks and turning points of life, my little case remained with me as I shifted from property to property. I rarely thought of it, but was always careful to keep it tucked away in the safest of places.

Two years after pulling the pin on playing the game and caring excessively about the results of matches, a group of East End factory lads applied copious amounts of peer pressure and eventually roped me into joining a team, thanks primarily to their mission statement.

The ambition laid out to me as part of their pitch was that the team would be essentially non-competitive. The games were to be played amidst hysterical laughter, with pints and not points the focus. I kind of liked the sound of that and joined on the proviso that should I see any member of the team engaged in anything that looked like trying or an act of defensive desperation, I was out.

We all had a good laugh about my insistence, yet I was deadly serious inside.

Many of the lads had suffered tough times. There were mental health challenges that had been conquered, others ongoing and all of us had financial pressures from which our little team would hopefully provide some respite.

I've watched thousands of football matches over the years, both live and on television, and seen just about every standard that the game has to offer. Yet I can honestly say that we were the most misguided, loose and hilariously unprofessional football team I have ever seen on a pitch.

And I loved every minute of it.

The matches were of the poorest standard, with the odd moment of accidental skill, and the characters involved utterly manic and distracted. However, that mattered little, with the extended social activities the most attractive part of the association.

In fact, the body I now own in middle age is a testament to the years of committed service our team dedicated to the local establishment.

Just 400 yards from West Ham United's home ground at Upton Park sat the Boleyn Tavern, not the slick and refurbished disgrace that now occupies the space, but a gloriously traditional and embracing pub that truly became a second home.

Today, the new version sits within view of the now demolished ground and the considerable housing and retail development that began there in 2017. However, in days gone by, it was the pre- and post-match gathering point for many Hammer fans and the site of many of those head-butts I mentioned a little earlier.

It was also the chosen waterhole for our team, a collection of idiots from right around the globe who gathered there to watch, talk and analyse football.

We had a Scotsman named Kenny whose accent was so thick and coarse that I generally found myself laughing along with his stories, despite being completely unable to comprehend a word he had actually said. There was a five-foot-two Irishman, a Welsh boiler-man who had the most beautiful baritone singing voice I have heard to this very day and two Jamaican guys who played on opposite sides of the field as attacking wingers.

The oddest of odd, Chris and Andy sat high on the pitch, never keen to cross halfway and defend, all the while shouting the names of famous Caribbean cricketers to each other. At the pub, they would constantly remind us all of their supposedly immense penises and regale us with tales of all the action they had managed between the sheets.

I never saw any of the lead-up to such action, but who am I to doubt?

We enjoyed the company of a short Afghani nicknamed 'Slush', and it occurs to me now that I never actually knew his real name or the reasoning behind his less formal moniker.

Our shot-stopper made some of the more insane goalkeeping characters seen in professional football look measured and controlled. He claimed to be a distant cousin of Ferenc Puskás and a Hungarian under-17 representative.

We all knew it was bullshit, yet loved him anyway. The entire playing squad struggled to remain composed when he charged towards the sphere each and every time, shouting "Puskás!!!" as he launched his foot into the ball.

Years later, we became aware of his tragic death in a bar fight in Newcastle. That night a group of now ex-players who had remained connected met for a quiet vigil, shared a pint and said goodbye to one of the nicest and funniest men you could ever meet.

The most measured and stable characters were probably the five of us that slugged out long days at the factory. The 'factory lads', as we were known, were usually the first to feel the dreariness of exhaustion around the reserved table we occupied and also the first to call things a night and head home.

The biggest hit with the girls was Cameron, an Australian. Waitresses would swoon over his accent and groups of girls in the bar would approach him as a gang, pin him down, and ask about kangaroos, Paul Hogan and other cringeworthy stereotypes.

More often than not, Cameron picked up a telephone number, snuck in a goodnight kiss, and then copped a rollicking lashing from Chris and Andy, who insisted that he didn't have the goods downstairs to do what was required and make the lady in question happy.

Days of factory life were followed by evenings at the boozer. Sunday nights with the lads meant far more than the games that preceded them. Whilst others may think little of the sometimes transient friendships developed in that environment, to me, the pub meant everything, with football the conduit to draw us all there.

As a now-orphaned only child, the moments before sleep during those years were often tinged with feelings of loneliness and sorrow. Then a flash of thought would steer the mind towards one of the boys, their stupidity, their comment or their comical performances on a football pitch.

Some might suggest an element of escapism in such a process and I would probably agree. Yet for a person carrying a vast and hollow emptiness, the friendships and interactions within that football team proved valuable and life-changing.

Of course, with the realities of family life and reluctant maturity comes a decrease in the frequency of opportunities for men to gather and drink beer in pubs. After four years together as a team, things began to change. Slush began popping kids out at a rapid rate, Cameron headed back to Oz after his work contract ended, and three or four others started families around the same time.

I remained a staple at the 'table of knowledge' with a handful of others, until romance was to unexpectedly strike, something I'd always perceived as highly unlikely considering my natural scepticism around family life.

I guess what you grow up with either drives you to emulate that reality or encourages you to create something in stark contrast. For me, the choice was quite easy.

Life together has been nothing but beautiful ever since the day I used my beer goggles expertly and spotted my wife Janice across the room at a friend's wedding. I was a bumbling romantic and an emotional idiot, yet thankfully, so was Janice.

It was a perfect fit.

Both parties brought significant baggage to the relationship, yet perhaps that empathy for circumstances and memory has sustained the union for over 25 years. Rarely a harsh word has been uttered, three kids have arrived and even the biggest secret of all was eventually shared.

None of the joy, love nor our children, Iris, Matthew and Lauren, would have been possible without the healing and absolution that was engendered by those footballing mates. That world taught me much about life, love and community, provided some sense of stability and a confidence that led to the courage required to become a good father and a loving husband.

It is my greatest achievement.

Football has had such an ever-changing role in my life. Initially a playing obsession, then a desperate search for meaning, security and community and now, post 50, a metaphor.

With our children heading off to find their own places in the world and the manic realities of parenthood lessening somewhat over the last few years, football has perhaps never been more under my microscope.

But it looks different. More poignant and powerful.

I've only contact with two of the lads from the team, both family men and still living in London. Janice and I headed further afield, to Torquay and all its magnificence, the place where our tent was destined to be pegged.

Devon is a proverbial million miles from London, yet with new friends, our family and football, it has provided the very same stable base that the East London lunatics did all those years ago.

Sitting quietly at Plainmoor and watching the Torquay United Gulls fills my heart with joy. I go alone, silently, and sit remotely to hear the game as much as I watch it. Around two and a half thousand people share a similar experience, a far cry from Anfield or the London Stadium. However, with the wisdom of time now informing my view, there is no other place I would rather be.

It is a scene of purity and integrity: young semi-professional players seeking paths to future success and other men seemingly extending their passion for playing the game as far as it can possibly be stretched.

For near on 40 years I have been a hardworking, beer-swilling, West Ham- and England-supporting football fan. During that time, the game has been a challenge, a passion and then finally a saviour.

Now I see football as a representation of the universality of humanity. Its redemptive power alludes to just what we could be should hate and division be jettisoned and an acceptance of diversity be adopted by all.

That football metaphor is one that captures the powerful, emotional and inherent good that exists within people and the manner in which all three play out within the most popular sport on the planet.

As a result, it matters little to me who wins or loses these days, more what the game means to us all—the human stories that emerge.

It took me almost my whole life to date to grasp that concept. For me, one final step was required before reaching such a place of understanding and contentment, where the past could be shelved completely.

Unfortunately, it was destined to be uncomfortable.

Part of the attraction of the property Janice and I purchased in Torquay was the considerable garage on the south side of the house. Now dabbling in woodwork, there was ample space for me to set up the necessary equipment and after the heating was installed, it allowed for activity even on the most frigid of winter days.

Both cars were generally street parked and the garage housed a mountain of junk, old furniture, bric-a-brac and items surplus to requirements. My little case of footballers had been placed in a small plastic tub on the bottom level of some metallic shelving.

Above were Christmas decorations, an obsession of Janice's and one I have been happy to let her enjoy on her own. On a crisp, early December morning in 2012, Janice rummaged her way through the decorations, preparing them for entry to the house.

She diligently unravelled the lights, dusted off the baubles and inserted new batteries into the array of novelty items she had picked up over the years.

She also found a small, dusty case on the lowest shelf and opened it.

The side door creaked as it closed and Janice walked into our lounge room as I continued working on a crossword puzzle that had had me stumped for over three days.

"Johnny, what's this?" she asked, simply and kindly.

I'm pretty sure my bum left the lounge chair before I had fully rotated my neck to see what she was holding. I leapt across the room, snatched the box from her hands and shouted, "Fucking give that to me!"

I stormed off down the hallway, heading nowhere in particular and in a state of absolute panic.

Janice persisted. "Johnny, what is it? What's wrong?"

"Nothing. It's fucking nothing, alright! Just go away, leave me alone! It's nothing!"

The chase continued around the house for a few more minutes, with drenching rain preventing an escape to the outdoors. Eventually, Janice had me pinned up against the kitchen sink.

"What the hell is wrong, Johnny? Cut the swearing and grow up." She stared at me. "What are you hiding? I'm scared."

I didn't say a word.

There was a true sense of fear and desperation in Janice's voice before she asked, "What are those little things in there?"

It was at that point I realised the 40-year-old padlock had failed miserably and that Janice had already seen the contents of the case. The secret was out.

I hurled the case across the room. It smashed into the side of the fridge, strewing the contents right across the kitchen, as I skipped up the stairs three at a time and fled to our bedroom.

I lay there sobbing for what seemed an eternity, before the most beautiful woman in the world appeared bedside. Janice calmly gathered up 54 strange-looking little men and re-stacked them neatly into the case, climbed the stairs and now sat on the edge of the bed.

"Johnny, I don't know what this is and don't need to know if you don't want to tell me," she said without one iota of judgement or anger.

I rolled over and exposed the wetness of tears that were probably destined to be released at some stage. She was utterly stunned and threw her arms around me.

"Oh Johnny, I love you. What can I do?"

It was at that point that 34 years of secrecy ended. I pulled Janice up alongside me on the bed and placed the box between us. I told her about the wardrobe, the art and craft supplies, the hiding places and the journey the case had been on since 1978. I didn't need to say a word about the purpose, I could see the understanding in her eyes.

Janice understood the escape, the dreams, the pain and the purpose. She also understood why I was always organising get-togethers with friends, obsessed with the family being together on significant days and the happiest when in the company of fellow football fans and talking about the game.

She understood that unlike the present day, where I had intentionally surrounded myself with good friends and family and kept in contact with football people from the past who provided me with so much, the little boy inside that case had no-one.

All he had was a collection of shabbily crafted footballers that he loved, symbolic of the other world of which he dreamed and the people with which he so desperately wanted to fill his life.

The explanation took hours and Janice sat, listening intently from beginning to end. We ordered food that night, as we both forgot about everything else while a lifetime of memories were released. In the weeks that followed, I would have been happy to bin the case, having made something of a peace with the past and broken the shackles of regret. Yet Janice would have none of it.

My 54 little footballers now sit proudly on the mantel. Each Christmas they are a topic of conversation with our children and their families, yet something of a pain in the neck to dust.

It is a long journey from the rough and tumble of the East End of London to Torquay, from a frightened little boy to a husband, father and grandfather. That journey played a key role in my shift in mindset from a youthful competitive outlook on football to an appreciation of the eloquent power of the game and its redemptive qualities.

Those little men were my friends. Knowing they were always there potentially saved me as I struggled to find real ones early in life. They have been there almost every step of my football and life journey, one that has been worth it in every way.

CARLA,
AGE 24

Once you see past the roundabouts and politicians, Canberra is actually a pretty nice place.

Sure, there are Arctic events in winter, horrifically scorching summers and a landscape that looks like it has been abused by both, yet Australia's capital has far more to it than many people suggest. I've never really understood the anti-Canberra comments made by visitors from other parts of the country. It always seemed like there was some sort of superiority complex at play, or perhaps an inferiority one.

Mum and Dad set up digs there in the 1970s, in what would also become my home. Before that, they'd spent much of their early lives on the south coast of New South Wales. Mum was and is a free-spirited, tennis-playing storyteller, who to this very day holds attention in a room like few others I know.

Dad has always been very different. A quiet, reserved and considered man. Rarely a word escapes his lips without the consequences of their delivery having been considered. Sent off to boarding school in Sydney for his secondary education, his passion for rugby union, cricket and athletics was born and nurtured in the rough and tumble of an all-boys school environment.

Spending that time in a Catholic institution run by a now seriously discredited order of Brothers meant Dad saw and heard of things that a boy of that age should never. To this day the subject is a little taboo, with the scars of the 1970s still affecting him and thousands of other former students, right across Australia. It is likely that his passion for sport was built partly from a natural and instinctive love of competition, but also as a distraction from what was clearly an abusive and disgusting institution.

Whilst Mum was busy whacking tennis balls across a net as quite a promising young player, Dad was playing as a half-back in the school rugby team and building quite a reputation as an elusive and effective organiser. There was really no other role for Dad to fill on a rugby field. He is short and was subsequently chased around ovals by much larger men on a week-to-week basis, all hoping to bash the snot out of him before he was able to set up a try or score one of his own. Most of the time, they never quite managed to get their hands on him and his reputation grew. He also clubbed a few cricket balls around in the summer season and developed a strong passion for swimming and running.

After returning to the family home post high school graduation, reconnecting with the local community and meeting Mum in the process, Dad's sporting interests soon steered away from team environments and quickly morphed into a lifelong dedication to triathlons. Cycling eventually became his addiction and therapy.

To this day, Dad is running, riding and swimming each week, albeit a little more slowly now as he passes 60 and heads towards retirement.

No doubt, a love of the cycling-friendly open roads of southern Canberra and the affordability of new homes built on the then relatively new housing estates were both driving factors in Mum and Dad's decision to peg their tent in Calwell, ACT. They, like so many other young couples, wanted to build a life. Subsequently, that suburb became the foundation around which mine would also begin.

My older brother Tom preceded me, and we were strangely born on the same day—July 17. As if to prove the old saying of the apple never falling very far from the parental tree, Tom was to inherit and perhaps even surpass his father's level of passion for sport and just about every game that human beings play competitively.

To say Tom loves sport is like suggesting that Canberra's politicians occasionally lie. Enjoying a school life somewhat similar to Dad's, he played pretty much everything he possibly could and became an excellent cricketer and proficient footballer at Marist College Canberra.

Now in his late 20s and with a family of his own that makes finding time for personal participation somewhat tricky, Tom watches/monitors sport 24 hours a day. Frankly, I'm not quite sure where he even finds the time to build the database of facts, results and statistics that lives in his head.

How he completes the jobs he is required to do at his place of employment is also a bit of a mystery, but they keep paying him, so he must be getting something done.

He and Dad together in the same room can become a living nightmare, unless Mum can manage to steer the conversation towards something far more to her liking, such as family, reality television or cushions. My mum has a strange obsession with cushions that remains undiagnosed to this very day.

Cricket remains a passion of Tom's, yet his biggest challenge is keeping up with football matches from around the globe. As many Australians will understand, the Land Down Under is in potentially the worst possible global time zone when it comes to viewing prime-time events held in Europe and the United States.

As a Liverpool fan, Tom has spent many a dark and cold Canberra night under the doona, phone in hand, whilst the men in red do battle with some of Europe's best. Yet he also needs to keep abreast of the remainder of the English Premier League action, as well as World Cups, European Championships and other significant international tournaments.

When major tennis, golf, cycling and athletics events are underway, they too are watched in the wee hours by a brother who must seriously be under suspicion of being a vampire. Wallabies' matches are not negotiable when the team is abroad, no matter the hour, and even full days of Test cricket will not stop his determination to consume sport at what often appears an unhealthy level.

Somehow, he crawls off to work in the morning, often with little or no sleep and destined to produce another amazing feat of concentration and commitment the very next night. The obsession has forged a father/son connection that many others would envy, perhaps even me at times. Yet Dad and I have bonded in a slightly different way.

I grew up expected to be what many in the past would have termed a traditional and typical young Australian girl. However, these days, I guess there is actually no such thing. The Barbie dolls rolled in at birthdays, pretty bows were placed in my hair and I always felt surrounded by pink clothes.

As an adult, I now realise that none of that was me; more perceptions of what a girl is supposed to be, by well-meaning relatives and friends.

Luckily, as someone inherently different to that stereotype and the perceptions that more and more modern young women continue to challenge, my youth coincided with a growing trend towards young girls taking up football. As a rather coarse stereotype of the past, most had viewed female football

WHEN MUM AND DAD SEE ME KICK

players through a rather narrow and limited lens, with the description of 'short-haired lesbians' accurately capturing the picture that existed in the minds of most Australians.

Whilst there was some logical basis for those views, it was completely irrelevant to me as a young girl, something I had never heard or considered. In fact, when Dad first raised the idea of having a go at football, I'm not too sure I even knew what a lesbian was.

Initially, it just sounded like a silly idea. I'd seen people playing the game in parks and a little bit on television, yet had no idea of the rules, other than the fact that the use of hands was not permitted.

Then, what started out as an adventure with social benefits actually became something much, much more. Looking back, it strikes me that football played quite a transformative role, gave me plenty of enjoyment and helped forge a wonderful relationship with my dad.

My football career did not exactly start smoothly, with some initial reluctance to the idea as a six-year-old. I am pretty sure there may even have been a few tears, yet Mum and Dad rightfully felt certain that physical exertion and involvement in a team sport were good things for any young person in the process of picking up the necessary life skills.

I can still vividly remember the trip to a well-known sports store to lace on my first pair of football boots and thinking that they not only looked silly, but were the most uncomfortable things I had ever worn. That view quickly changed when I was given a ridiculously over-sized yellow team shirt and a pair of shorts that extended well below my knees. As an ensemble, it made me look like something of a destitute cartoon character, whose parents had grabbed the most colourful items they could find at the local opportunity shop, in a clear effort to intentionally send their child out into the world to be bullied.

I am not sure whether I had the word in my vocabulary at such an early age, but if I did and also possessed the courage to use it, I would simply have said, "What the fuck am I doing?"

I looked and felt like an idiot, but like millions of young girls around the globe who have fallen for the game, football was to quickly lure me in.

Not that I was particularly sure of exactly what was going on during that first season. After a 20-minute drive to a windswept and freezing south Canberra park, Sunday mornings became something very much like the *Lord of the Flies*, with the frigid and extreme conditions requiring survival and not a single person at the venue appearing happy to be there.

Mums and dads clenched their hands around cups of tea and coffee. Beanies were a non-negotiable for everyone except the players and the rare few arriving without a scarf were quickly regretting their stupidity and destined for the most uncomfortable of mornings.

Tom and his mates were fine. Along with a few older siblings dragged along for the pain, they set off immediately as a group. On a nearby and vacant field, they would chase, tackle and trip each other for an hour, before returning to their parents with all sorts of cuts and injuries.

I can still clearly recall the parents and players standing in large groups, huddled up and giggling as kick-off approached. They were awaiting the arrival of the coach, as he dragged himself and the training gear across from an adjacent car park.

Our mentor was always a little late. Years later, I discovered that many of the parents who had spent Saturday evenings down at the local sports club with him were well aware why he arrived a little under the weather each and every Sunday morning.

At some point a football would appear and, as a team, we would complete the most simplistic and inane warm-up. Then a tall person blew a whistle and the chaotic chase for a ball around a paddock began. Even that is perhaps a rather generous way to describe what was in fact mayhem—unstructured, tactic-less, and bizarre mayhem that appeared to have two clear effects.

Firstly, the kids transformed into what could easily have been described as cocaine-fuelled Rottweilers, frantically searching for that rare moment when the ball would fall perfectly for them and trickle slowly towards their favoured foot.

It is at that point where small children's football brains malfunction and any instruction from the coach that may have been handed out at training during the week is forgotten in an instant. Thoughts of attempting to do anything less primal than striking the ball with as much force possible and with utter disregard for its destination are simply out of the question.

For beginning footballers, the idea of kicking the ball as hard, high, and far as humanly possible is the fundamental objective, with the only variation being if a goal mouth is in sight.

The chaos also breeds parental insanity, as they morph into something other than their normal selves. Basically, they cease to be calm adults who are supposed to be present for the lovely social interaction that kids' sport often provides and transform into cheerleading lunatics whose children must apparently walk away from the park in triumph—or else.

Despite the fact that the players were so utterly fixated by the ball and moving as a pack from one side of the pitch to the other, unlikely to be able to comprehend and react to any advice from the sidelines, parents and guardians still felt the need to shout out the most useless advice to their daughters.

To prove the point, I'm quite certain that I never really heard or comprehended a word shouted in my direction whilst playing, yet did quietly observe some seriously over-zealous parents when it was my time to take a break.

I have often wondered just how hopeless they were as footballers. I've also considered whether the somewhat comical and outrageous scene we created was near the worst example of football on the planet or exactly the same as the early experiences of some of Australia's greatest players.

Perhaps it is somewhere in between.

Thankfully, football does become a little more structured the older one gets. As our team improved, so did the level of pleasure I took from the game. By the time our ages reached double figures, the mass huddle that saw very few opportunities on goal had been replaced by the rough definition of positions and an increased awareness of the players as to exactly what their role was.

I ended up in defence. Without the fleet of foot required to dazzle opponents and score frequent goals, it was wisely suggested that I use my size and strength to deny others. It was a role I actually became quite good at.

We even managed to earn a few trophies over the years, although sometimes it was difficult to tell which ones were for actually winning something and which may have been merely a product of the 'everyone wins a prize' culture that has now entrenched itself in kids' sport. Whilst many see such a trend as potentially damaging to kids as they grow older, the game itself taught me more than enough lessons without even considering the rewards that may have been handed to me for playing it.

With a sustained belief that I was something of a misfit and unable to conform to the expected female stereotype from a young age, finding other ways to express myself was important. It was also a struggle at times, and I'll be forever grateful to football for providing me with that opportunity. If it had not come along, I am not sure what else might have grabbed my interest and become my sport of choice.

What I find most appealing about the game is the expression within it. The first time I did put my foot forcefully through a ball with all the naivety and innocence of that first season, a statement was made. It was a statement of achievement, defiance and of belonging. It also brought commendation from Mum and Dad, which was kind of cool at the time.

After seeking a sense of place and community and struggling to find it in the activities undertaken by many young girls, I could now inform people that I was a footballer. It was such a clear and definitive statement, one that everyone requires a version of in order to build a confidence in identity, as they seek to discover exactly who they are.

That confidence can take many years to build and football helped forge it in me, despite a multitude of other personal challenges along the way. The fact that a few princesses at school felt football was still a game reserved for butch, gay women made it even more attractive to me. To those of us who think a little differently to the norm, the idea of being countercultural is actually appealing.

With Tom and Dad continuing their nightly recaps of sporting events played around the globe and an undoubted common interest, football became Dad's and my special time together. He was probably the least vocal of those aggressive parents on the sideline, yet the most supportive and also completely aware that my playing the game was doing a whole lot more for me than many would have realised.

He even coached us for a season or two and we had the odd dustup in the car on the way home after his moody teenage daughter turned on the attitude. Yet the enhanced relationship was a direct result of the game and something not all members of the team enjoyed.

Football also taught me much about conflict, the simple fact that life will present it in spades and that one's approach to it is crucial.

When an opposition player first decided to make a physical statement and gave me an almighty whack well off the ball, I cowered like a baby, hurt, and embarrassed. I am not too sure at which age I eventually found the courage to stand my ground and return serve, but I did and rarely lost a physical battle over the remainder of my career.

WHEN MUM AND DAD SEE ME KICK

Looking back, it strikes me that I came across some very hard and physical players. In the old days, men would have referred to them as bitches.

Thankfully, such gendered language is slowly being erased and female footballers at the top level can now play the game increasingly unfettered and unconcerned by misogynist thinking.

Hopefully, removing those falsehoods around female sexuality, politeness and aggression will never define the narrative in the women's game again. My nieces are counting on it.

These days I fill the stereotype of a female footballer quite well, despite no longer playing the game competitively. I prefer a beer to a cocktail, women rather than men, and advocate strongly for the LGBTIQ+ community, as well as young people who remain challenged by outdated notions of identity.

From a kid who was never satisfied playing with dolls, dancing in a troupe, or investing her hard-earned money in make-up and fashion, I became the woman I am today, thanks to a couple of great parents, a terrific brother and the freedom of expression that football encouraged.

That freedom is something I often speak about with friends, family, and the younger women I know.

Just like I needed a bit of a nudge from Dad, maybe a few of them need a word or two of advice from someone who has lived the journey.

The best part of all was that Dad was there at every step, every fork in the road, every injury, every tear and every trophy, watching his little girl break free of what others may have hoped she would be. The game brought us closer together, forging a sustainable relationship upon which we both now lean when required.

Football taught me much about life, conflict, relationships and who I am at my core.

Hopefully, future generations of women will have things easier than the 20th century pioneers. As I read more and more about the origins of the women's game in Australia, it is clear to me that they did it tough. Their journey and battle for respect and acceptance was much more difficult than mine.

Yet there is still a little way to go before we arrive at a place where equal training, equal effort and equal skill result in equal coverage and equal pay. Am I confident women's football will eventually get to that point? I'm not too sure.

But I will be watching every minute of that evolution, probably propped up on the lounge next to Tom and Dad and enjoying the fact that when I make a comment about the game, it is treated with the same respect and value as one of their own.

In my view, that is where it all starts and I am lucky to have the two of them in my life.

TRAVIS,
AGE 28

Nine months into a full rehabilitation of my left knee, I'd had just about enough.

When the joint fails, anterior cruciate ligament snapped in two and surgery required, the stark reality of what that means for a sportsperson is confronting and sometimes, overwhelming. Nothing can quicken the long road back to full fitness and the psychological challenges faced on the journey are as significant as the obvious physical ones.

In the oddest of ironies, a team player instantly becomes a solo artist, removed from the comfort of the dressing room and forced to operate alone during the early stages of rehabilitation. The relationships that previously offered support and strength become more distant, with the recovery process a lonely one filled with frustration and doubt.

My injury occurred playing football on a wet and frigid afternoon in Sydney, Australia, in a National Premier League fixture, as the end of a long season approached. Mid-table and without relegation concerns, the match itself meant little, with both sides going through the motions as the game petered out late, before eventually ending in a scoreless draw.

To an observer, the match was far from entertaining to watch. A forlorn attacking midfielder left prostrate on the pitch in a ball of agony with around ten minutes remaining on the referee's timepiece could well have been the most dramatic moment of the entire contest.

A long angled ball had been played towards the grandstand side wing; I chested it down nicely and took control at my feet. With a defender seeking to close down the space, a quick step-over and a subsequent dart towards midfield appeared to be the best option available, one I'd taken many times before.

However, on this occasion, the moment weight landed on my left leg, something frighteningly audible and painful brought what was meant to be a short and decisive run to a halt before it had even started.

I will never forget the 'pop' that echoed from well inside the knee joint. For those who have experienced the same, an understanding of just how gruesome and concerning the sound actually is needs little explanation and cannot be understated. As with all injuries, shock sets in and my first recollection is of being hopeful that as unusual as the moment had felt, the pain was surely to be temporary.

In the 20 to 30 seconds that followed, the more logical side of the brain kicked in. I had heard about the 'popping' sound from other players, seen teammates go down with ACL injuries in the past and began to come to the realisation that making it to work on Monday morning was unlikely.

That was confirmed when an effort to stand brought immense pain and a buckling through my left leg that was probably enough for any competent doctor to diagnose the seriousness of the injury right on the spot.

I've never been that good at reading people's faces in different social circumstances. Apparently, my girlfriend Kim was desperately keen for me to ask her out for over two years before I finally received the tip-off from a friend that encouraged me to do so. However, the look on the club physio's face as she checked the stability of the joint in the change room a few minutes later was telling and compellingly hopeless.

Rather pointlessly, I checked with her anyway. "It's fucked, isn't it?"

"Yeah, well and truly. We better get you in to see a specialist as soon as possible. You're going under the knife, Trav."

That news brought nothing but fear. Somehow I had avoided major football injuries throughout my career. A broken thumb at 12, a bruised shoulder whilst playing for a school team at 16, and thousands of cuts, scratches and bruises to my feet and shins had been the worst of it.

As I sat alone in the change room with a throbbing knee and the thought of a ruined off-season, little did I know just how inconvenient injured life was to become, or how busy I was to be over the next few days.

The first phone call required was to Andy, manager of the parks and recreation crew at the local council.

With evening trainings and weekend matches, 6 a.m. starts at the council are a perfect fit for a semi-professional footballer in Australia. The Monday following my injury, the intention had been to prune a 60-metre stretch of beautiful white rose bushes that grew on the median strip adjacent to the local hotel.

Andy had set me the same task in the two preceding years, becoming aware of a love of horticulture that had been developed as a child after spending time with my grandmother. School holidays were spent learning as much as I could about the thousands of plants she maintained on her property in Mittagong, New South Wales.

Whilst most of the council boys were usually off on ride-on mowers and attacking the thick and weedy grasses in local parks, Andy appreciated my attention to detail and gifted me a host of more delicate jobs that required a little skill and subtlety.

Sadly, the roses would be pruned by someone else this time around, with immediate sick leave applied for and an appointment made with a reputable knee specialist on the following Wednesday morning.

In what was always a handy bonus, the father of three junior players and a keen benefactor to the club was also a well-respected orthopaedic surgeon. He had been responsible for looking after a number of club players who had also experienced the misfortune of serious injury over the years and by all accounts was top-notch in his trade.

Armed with a pair of crutches acquired from a local discount chemist and driven to the appointment by an Uber driver who could not have been more helpful in getting a crippled athlete in and out of what was a small car, I sat silently in a sterile waiting room. I foolishly prayed that the diagnosis would stun medical science and have the surgeon screaming "It's a miracle" like a crazed American televangelist.

Sadly, I was as boring as could be and the most classic open-and-shut case of a snapped anterior cruciate ligament that had ever been seen.

Luckily, the man charged with opening up flesh and using a section of ligament from my hamstring to act as a new ACL would fit me into his schedule the following Monday.

The five days that followed were a nightmare of worry and anticipation.

My mobile phone pinged all day and most of the night, with messages of best wishes from teammates designed to get me up for the fight ahead. The most compelling were from players who had also suffered extended periods on the sideline after major surgery.

The club's first grade goalkeeper had undergone shoulder reconstructions to both joints and understood exactly what the next year would entail. After hopping across the room and crashing onto the lounge after one of many uncomfortable trips to the bathroom in my rather cramped and cluttered unit, his Saturday night message hit home.

"Trav, there will be a time when you want to give up. Don't. It's gonna hurt and you're gonna hurt. Show 'em how tough you are. Dave."

Initially, I thought his words were a little dramatic. Sure, we have all seen stories of athletes and their struggles in returning from significant injury, yet was this message from a mate perhaps overstating things a little, especially from a psychological perspective?

I was soon to find out.

Yet before the good doctor was to slice me open and get to work, the small matters of health insurance and a hospital stay needed sorting. After nearly choking on a KitKat whilst reading the official correspondence from the surgeon in regards to the cost of the actual procedure, those feelings turned to anger when the estimated compensation from my long-term health fund was discovered.

I sincerely apologise to the lovely young woman at the fund who passed the figure on to me over the phone. I try not to swear where possible, yet knowing that any chance of a holiday for Kim and I was off the cards for at least the next few years caused me to let fly with a common expletive.

There was also the issue of a return to work.

Unfortunately, the nature of my position at the council meant there was no chance of a return to office duties or a lateral shift into a different role, as my knee began to heal in the early months of recovery. That meant a dependence on the income protection insurance I had been urged to take out by my father some years earlier; in retrospect, one of the best decisions I have ever made.

A month of accrued sick leave and three months of paid leave via the insurance company would allow me to commit totally to the rehabilitation process, and as it turned out, read a hell of a lot of great books along the way.

I will admit to having a little sook on the Tuesday evening before the surgery. I was nervous, depressed and scared of what lay ahead. Kim sat with me into the early hours of the morning before I finally crashed through sheer exhaustion and was able to bin the normal human apprehension around operations and exactly what life would look like afterwards.

As is the case with medical procedures, men and women in white coats zipped around the room, friendly conversations were had and the always fun task of selecting the pre-op music fell to the patient. I went with the Foo Fighters, thinking that anything too soppy might simply heighten emotion and that David Grohl thrashing away might put me in the best state of mind, for what was merely the first step in the long journey that awaited.

Then, blank.

Post-operative recovery is one that presents the patient in the most humorous of lights. Kim informed me days later of some of the gibberish I came up with in the hours after coming to. Of course, I have no memory of it, but she still laughs at my dazed and bumbled marriage proposal, delivered with one eye closed and lips barely able to construct the words required.

"Kim, you know wwwwwhat?.......One day.......we sssssshould get maaaaarried."

Rather cleverly, Kim reminds me of this drunken promise on a regular basis and I just cannot see any way out of the deal.

Within 24 hours of the surgery being completed, I was wishing for a return to the operating theatre, merely for some relief from the agonising pain that set in. My God, it hurt.

The pain was like something I had not felt before: a deep and intense stabbing and throbbing that came together in waves, along with a constant and restrictive soreness that combined to create what can only be described as torture.

With an intention of avoiding painkillers where possible, my naivety was apparent almost immediately and the pills were washed down as soon as the anaesthetic began to wear off. They were to become a staple over the next two to three weeks at home, something that would previously have sat uncomfortably with me, knowing the dangers of strong prescription drugs.

However, looking back, the idea of living those first few days without something to allow for sleep and at least some relief from the excruciating pain seems almost insane.

As did the request of a nurse who waltzed into my room on the Friday morning following the operation and suggested that we try to stand up and shuffle about a little on what was essentially a new knee.

I responded to the request rather rudely: "Are you friggin' kidding?"

The nurse was not, and a detailed explanation of the common practice of getting ACL patients up and moving as quickly as possible was dished out before I somehow managed to stand upright. As a slow-moving duo, we made it to the door of the hospital room, managed to cross the width of the hallway, touched the opposite wall and then returned to the safety of my bed.

After awkwardly propping back up against the pillows and giving the attractive nurse a flash of everything I had under my gown, I felt as though I had run a marathon.

It was the first time that Dave's words really struck home. All of a sudden, I knew exactly what he meant.

Life moves pretty slow for the athlete stumbling around his unit with crutches, able to do little more than sit lifelessly on the lounge, watching television, making phone calls or playing Xbox. Frankly, I was bored within days and expressed that feeling to Mum during her nightly check-up via Skype.

The following morning, she arrived with a cardboard box that was dropped with a thud on my 1970s retro dining table.

"What's that?" I asked.

"It's a box of books, Trav; thought you might like to take up reading while you recover."

Now, it is fair to say that the last book I had read probably contained less than 500 words and plenty of pictures. Far from an academic, I had struggled at school, with English perhaps the most significant of the challenges I faced.

Some old biddy with a bun in her hair had tried to get me fascinated by an Australian poet named Bruce Dawe. I do remember that. As well as a freaky, bearded, red-haired Year 12 teacher who seemed to do a wobbly every time he read William Wordsworth to a class of mostly cackling 17-year-old boys.

Aside from those two memories, the notion of reading literature and enjoying it was so foreign to me that, on the outside, Mum's plan could well have appeared as one of the silliest she had ever concocted.

After a cup of tea, a brief chat and an explanation of the upcoming physiotherapy trips to which I would require a lift, she left and I hopped over to the box of books.

There were a few football titles, as well as around 15 novels I had never even heard of, let alone laid eyes on before. An image of two boys leaping from a pier into the water with a beautiful sunset behind them caught my eye.

Cloudstreet, by Tim Winton.

Whilst my poor effort and limited achievements in English at school could have potentially seen my reading ability suffer, scouring football results and stories in the sports section of the newspaper had potentially saved me. Rather pleased, I quickly realised that the prose was not beyond me.

I wedged my back into the corner of the lounge, propped my busted limb up on the cushions to my left and read the opening passages of the novel. Three hours later and 120 pages in, I emerged. Wow, I was hooked.

Mum had nailed it, both in making those early months of recovery far more bearable, and discovering within me a passion for books and reading that continues to this day.

Early physio sessions were tedious. With so little movement in the joint and a steady-as-she-goes approach required, there were days where a pointlessness seemed to exist in the making of the trip at all.

It was simply astonishing just how small the required movements were and how difficult they were to perform accurately. Beads of sweat would trickle down my forehead, as I pushed as hard as I could, encouraged by a physio well aware that my desire to return to an elite level was simply a no-brainer.

Progress was slow, very slow, yet did eventually come and the idea of jogging kept resurfacing in my head. Thankfully, I was talked out of attempting to do so on a weekly basis by a professional who had seen the impatience of athletes many times before. He emphasised the importance of doing things right rather than quickly when it came to knee reconstructions.

Post physio sessions, I immersed myself in reading. Time flew during *The Great Gatsby, Catch-22* and *The Colour Purple*. Winton had really grabbed my attention and *The Riders* was one of the most amazing novels I have read, despite being completely unaware of precisely what occurred at the end. I'm still trying to work it out.

After the initial loosening up of the joint and re-establishing some freedom of movement, the next phase was walking and becoming accustomed to the structural changes inside my knee. When the physio said walk a kilometre, I did one with a few hundred metres tacked on, and as each phase of rehabilitation came around, a policy of 'everything plus another 20 per cent' became my mantra.

I wanted to be back on the pitch as soon as possible. With the injury occurring in August and a new NPL season beginning in March of the following year, I rather ambitiously set my sights on a Round 1 return. By Christmas, it became clear that a more realistic time frame was sometime in May, smack-bang in the middle of the season.

Alarmingly, I jumped on the bathroom scales on Boxing Day, after gorging on Christmas lunch with family, and did not appreciate the result. Eight kilos had been added thanks to immobility and even the light walking and hand weights I had begun doing at home were in no way enough to counteract the amount of food I'd become used to consuming as a footballer.

A slow realisation developed. Even when given the green light to recommence running and full training, there could well be weeks or months of effort required before being able to return to my previous playing weight.

Along with the expected psychological challenge of believing in the knee and trusting its stability, it was also becoming clear that selection in the starting 11 by May was far from a certainty.

Dave had been correct in the most part. The knee had hurt immensely, as had I, yet he was wrong about one thing. I never once thought of giving up.

The New Year brought the freedom of gentle sessions at the park, navigating traffic cones in a pattern designed to gradually build up strength in the knee. By that stage, the club physio had taken over the rehabilitation program and was building football specific movements into my daily routine.

In late January, 6 a.m. starts were back on the agenda as I returned to work.

Andy looked after me, as he always had, ensuring that the specific tasks I took on were comfortable and not likely to pose any danger. By February, I was losing weight, feeling stronger and had begun kicking a ball whilst on my daily walk.

Later that month, the all-clear was given to return to running. Whilst I had already snuck in a bit of light jogging in the month prior, the fact that it was now medically approved was like the proverbial red rag to a bull.

As many will know, the progress made in returning from a serious knee injury accelerates the further into the journey the person travels and within a few sessions, despite a little soreness in the evenings, I felt capable of running at around 80 per cent of capacity.

That quickly became 90 per cent and soon, unrestricted, despite a mental block existing around just how far the knee could be pushed in terms of changing direction and pushing off when at top speed. Alongside the excellent progress,

I was yet to fully extend the joint laterally and each time an attempt to do so was made, I bailed out.

It is difficult to describe the feeling. On one hand, logically knowing the strength of the new material in the knee and the extensive rehabilitation undertaken to make it function, and on the other, a real concern of hearing the 'pop' again and crumbling to the ground.

I texted Dave.

"Hi, mate, I'm all fixed up and free to train but my brain is holding me back. I can't trust it. Thoughts?"

His reply was probably not what I wanted to hear. "You have to, mate; once you have done it once, there is no stopping you. Are you tough or not?"

I asked Kim to join me at the park late that afternoon. Her job was to provide me with a long angled ball that I would gather on the sideline, just as I had done seconds before the knee had initially given way. My plan was to then recreate the steps that followed, turn sharply onto my left side and cut inside my imaginary defender.

Kim is a footballer herself and produced the perfect ball at the first attempt. I chested it down and then calmly controlled it before returning it to her some 30 metres away.

"What was that?" she said.

"Just not quite ready, babe. Go again." In truth, I was shaking like a leaf.

The next ball was as accurate as the first and I brought it down well, then pushed off from the right before planting my left foot in the turf, twisting and exploding into the imaginary midfield. There was no pain, no tightness and no sound.

Exhilarated, I dribbled 20 or so metres and thumped a ferocious left foot strike into the goal at the far end of the park, as Kim stood in midfield wondering what her idiot boyfriend was doing.

I'd like to say that the ball was collected from the net and followed by a proud and confident walk back to the centre of the pitch, where a gentle kiss was planted on Kim's lips. Instead, the ball needed to be rescued from a stormwater drain that ran parallel to the field, as the un-netted goal had seen it whizz through, clear a small wire fence and land in the slush that sat at the low point of the drain.

I hopped the fence with ease, tears building, retrieved the ball and hoofed it in the opposite direction with my left foot.

I sprinted back to Kim and realised why I loved her so much when she simply said, "You're back, baby."

That was late March, 246 days since I had collapsed on the pitch in agony.

With the new season underway and the team performing well, full training and participation in all sessions was now permitted. The kilos dropped quickly, fitness levels improved weekly and by the end of April, the coach had enquired as to how confident I was in returning.

Of course, no player would say anything other than yes when given the green light for selection. However, confidence is built over time and in terms of my body in full combat against actual opposition, I was as unconfident as one could be.

The night before my return, Kim and I watched *Love Actually*, a film so full of hope and positivity that it is difficult to navigate without a tear or two along the way. It was precisely what I needed heading into my first game of football in nearly ten months.

Bent over and lacing up my boots in the sheds prior to taking to the pitch, there were a few evil thoughts circling. Did I still have the speed that had served me well my entire career? Would one knock to the knee send me back to the operating table?

Or worse still, were the opposition determined to test out the joint with some physical stuff in the opening minutes?

Soon after kick-off, I picked up the ball on the wing and dribbled past one defender, before passing off to a teammate. I continued the run and received the ball back centrally, before sliding a pass through for our centre-forward, who had sadly drifted off-side.

At the end of the movement, I was clipped from behind and brought down aggressively by a thug of a central defender who was notorious for hacking away whenever his lack of speed saw him caught out.

As I gathered myself on the ground, a quick check confirmed that all had remained intact and that the knee had survived its first tumble without incident. As I returned to my feet, Dave strode confidently from his area to within earshot.

"Nice tackle, Herman Munster, you'll have to do better than that. He's a tough little bastard. You right, Trav?"

Only a thumbs-up was required and Dave shot a quick wink back in support.

That moment probably summed up why I love football so much.

From as early as three or four years of age, when a thirst for football comes to life in many young children, I had been gripped by the game. Running around with a smile and chasing a ball that felt so good when kicked simply engrossed me like no other activity.

The subsequent camaraderie, as well as a sense of team and club, built special friendships and connections that, frankly, negatively affected academic pursuits. However, those relationships also provided more intangible things that are probably worth a great deal more in the long run.

Nothing tests that reliance on teammates and community more than a serious injury that ostracises a player for an extended period of time. Within the strange irony, a footballer so dependent on teammates all of a sudden becomes focused on no-one but themselves out of necessity and in order to one day make it back into the team environment.

That experience added layers of perspective to my appreciation of the game. As did the chance to read the stories of Australian players and coaches like Johnny Warren, Ange Postecoglou and Craig Johnston whilst recovering. Mum knew that complete isolation from the game was probably a bad thing during rehabilitation, despite her obvious keenness to see me read at least something of literary merit.

All three of those men faced enormous challenges during their careers, with a resilience required in order to achieve what they eventually did. While my story is far removed from the legendary ones of Warren, Postecoglou, Johnston and many others, the metaphor of adversity and overcoming obstacles connects us. In my case, the goal was achieved via a supportive partner, a box of novels, a brilliant surgeon and a mountain of hard work.

Thousands of footballers have faced similar physical challenges and thousands more will do so in the future. Every single one of them will have dreams of playing the beautiful game again.

It will be the motivation to take to the pitch for just one more season that will hopefully enable them all to do so.

JULIETTE,
AGE 32

I sometimes wonder what my parents might have done with me had they known the stresses and challenges I would present to them later in life.

Hand in hand, they walked from the foyer of a Melbourne hospital with their new bundle of joy rugged up against the bitter cold of a typical June day. Most likely, they expected to take their little treasure home, get them settled into an effective routine and then begin to enjoy the lifelong journey ahead as a family. Billions have lived that very same scenario and billions more will do so in the future, most with something of a similarity in their stories. No doubt, my parents anticipated being just another set of parents, raising a well-adjusted child in the suburbs, and managing to provide a decent life and foundation for their little family.

And, on the outside, things actually started out quite normally.

Fortunately, I was a healthy baby, barring the odd asthma attack in the years that followed. In true Australian fashion, swimming lessons were undertaken to aid in the management of those breathing difficulties, and I became a heck of a swimmer.

Some of the fondest memories I have as a young child involve water. Swimming my heart out with Mum and Dad poolside, both sipping coffee and enjoying the successes of their offspring. School carnivals became a breeze, the medals were chalked up in brisk succession and the fitness level I achieved meant further successes in any activity that was heavily reliant on cardiovascular performance.

That base line level of fitness came in very handy when I first started playing football.

In search of a winter activity, my parents took me down to a local field for a brisk initiation to the game, hopeful that I would take an instant liking to it. It would be fair to say that I did not.

Within 15 minutes of arriving, while the kids were completing pretty basic drills with a coach they all appeared to know from the previous season, the loudest and most confident member of the group decided to play the clown. Rather than following instructions and completing the passing drill correctly by returning the ball to the coach, he decided to break ranks, turn 180 degrees and thump the ball directly towards the rest of us, who were patiently lined up waiting our turn.

Most saw it coming and reacted accordingly. However, as has often been the case in life, my mind had become preoccupied by other thoughts and I was oblivious to what was headed my way. The ball thumped into my face, subsequently breaking my nose and loosening a front tooth that required a few trips to the dentist in order to ensure its survival.

I was far from the toughest kid in the neighbourhood, but I can safely say that it hurt like hell and saw me fall to the ground with my hands clasped around my face. There was great concern, plenty of blood and the tears flowed.

That incident was my first experience of football and looking back, it is stunning that I decided to even give the game another chance just a few weeks later. It was with another club, however, as the utter embarrassment I felt and the kindness of my parents to understand those feelings meant I was spared the pain of returning as the boy with the busted nose who cried his eyes out like a girl.

If only they knew.

My new club was better, friendly and supportive, and the boys were great fun to be around. Most were not school friends, more a mishmash of kids from a variety of cultures and suburbs.

We had the son of a Scotsman, Chris, blessed with the social curse of ginger hair and freckles, as well as a couple of Italian kids who were excellent little footballers right from the start, and three Greek boys who all appeared determined to represent their home country at a World Cup one day.

Our goalkeeper was the captain of the team, the coach's son, and blessed with all the idiosyncrasies of a professional shot stopper. The most important member of our team was a lovely boy named Andrew, who suffered from what I now know to be cystic fibrosis.

After most games Andrew cried, such was the pain in his limbs. I'll never forget seeing his dad swoop him up in his arms, kiss him and carry him to the car like a small baby. He would lay Andrew on the back seat and, as I discovered a few years later, place his son in a therapeutic bath to help alleviate his discomfort as soon as they arrived home.

Having Andrew in our team taught us all something about tolerance, courage and difference. It also formed an important part of the memories upon which I would draw as my own identity became uncertain in the years that followed.

During a match on a freezing July morning in 2001, an opposition player challenged Andrew for the ball, won it and said "Thanks, spastic" as he dribbled away. The comment was a red rag to a bull and four or five of us ran at the offender instantly.

I'm not too sure what we all intended to do when we got there, yet our best midfielder Max arrived first and took care of the situation for us. He slid in violently and chopped both legs from under the abuser, as astonished parents gasped. It was the most violent tackle I have ever seen on a football pitch live and a red card was produced within seconds.

Whilst I'm not too proud of my feelings around that incident, I was glad he did it.

Later, Max told me that he copped an absolute hiding from his parents when he arrived home. They were rightfully embarrassed and furious. Max waited patiently for them to finish the dressing down before telling them the reason behind his action. To their credit as parents, they reinforced their disapproval around his decision to use violence as a response, yet also softened a little and explained how they understood why he had done what he did.

Not all Saturday mornings were so spicy. Mostly, we had a blast running around together, played some nice football and won more often than we lost. I was posted out on the left wing, destined to zip up and down that flank, constantly shifting from attack to defence. Scoring wasn't my thing. Whipping balls into the box to provide for others seemed to be my best asset.

The skills required to control the ball were nurtured over a few years of decent instruction and coaching, yet it was the fundamental ability to run all day long that made me valuable. Of course, football begins as something of a rabble for kids at a very young age. However, once the challenges of those formative years are met and passed, the game starts to open up as the beautiful endeavour that it is.

Whilst swimming success and a love of football continued between the ages of seven and 12, soon after I found myself utterly unfocused and completely unsure as to why.

I had stopped pushing myself to the limit in the pool, knowing full well that I had any opposition covered and that there appeared to be no need to do anything other than the bare minimum. On the football pitch, my performances declined, with the motivation to track back and defend seemingly gone. I essentially became a bludging attacker, happy to pick up a pass provided by the hard work of others, yet unprepared to do the same for anyone else.

There were a host of confusing thoughts rumbling around in my head at the time. Introversion had taken over, my parents were concerned and I'd copped a few beatings at school from boys who had correctly identified a softer side to me that led to them smelling blood in the water.

Behind closed doors I was in constant tears, confused and feeling trapped. The never-ending feeling of wanting to be somewhere and someone else woke me each day and was the last thing of which I thought before restless sleep.

The problem was, I had no idea where I wanted to go and who I wanted to be. At the time, just anywhere and anyone else would have been fine.

I had stopped looking at kids my own age in the same vein. Rather than seeing the boys I spent time with at school in the usual blasé way and as young men just like me, I had begun analysing their bodies and features more intently.

Such analysis and observation became more frequent and pointed over a period of months and eventually came to a head on a Friday night at the pool where I had swum for eight years. A series of informal races were run on that night each week and, despite my mind being a million miles from the water, I prepared to step up onto the blocks and swim an under 14s 50-metre freestyle race that I was almost certain to win.

Manufacturing my goggles into a comfortable position on my head, I caught sight of the boy in the lane alongside. Probably two years older than me, I was completely transfixed by him. His chiselled upper body, powerful quadriceps and eye-catchingly brief swimming trunks left little to the imagination.

I wanted to reach out and touch him, despite not knowing exactly why, and the beginning of an erection quickly became out of control. A mad dash for the toilets followed and I locked myself in a cubicle until things had subsided.

For a boy raised in the traditional way and one surrounded by the supposed normality of male adolescence, the idea of leering at another lad and becoming sexually aroused created a level of fear that cannot be described. There was no chance of expressing such a concern to my parents; the sheer terror of potential disapproval made that impossible.

Instead, I was to become one of the thousands of Australian people living a secret life, in fear of recrimination and judgement and one based purely on who we choose to love.

Living in a dark silence became my norm. I walked away from football and swimming, petrified that a repeat of those confronting feelings would occur. A faked chronic back injury was the official reason, yet in reality, a teenage boy was wandering through life in a cloudy stupor of uncertainty, without any support or reassurance.

Rather comically, I chose to embrace femininity, feeling assured that looking closely at girls would get me 'back on track'. There was plenty of good material around the house to reprogram what I had become convinced was a brain requiring rewiring.

Department store catalogues, fashion magazines and my father's subscription to a clean but saucy mainstream men's magazine all provided the chance for a stern analysis of the female form. It was the most naive of strategies and now, almost comical to reflect upon.

The juvenile plan came crashing back to earth in no time. No matter how many glossy magazines I flipped through or how many scantily clad models and actresses I set eyes on, the suave guy on the opposite page wearing a dark suit and brandishing an expensive watch became the subject of my interest.

It was somewhere during that period and at the age of 15 that I reconciled with an obvious preference for male companionship and love.

Life experience has taught me that for most young people grappling with sexuality, there is no one moment where the realisation strikes, more a gradual acceptance and making of peace with feelings that sadly cause great anguish and pain.

However, those innate feelings are actually the most natural thing in the world for the person experiencing them. I would wish the process on no one, yet also feel lucky to have eventually arrived at the conclusion of it a better and more rounded person.

After a litany of scans, X-rays and doctors' visits to investigate a fabricated back injury of which the science could find no trace, my parents ordered me back onto the pitch. Frankly, I'd preferred to have been anywhere else and after showing little of the energy and zip I had previously on the left side of attack, spent much of the remainder of the season sitting on a freezing cold metallic bench.

With headphones firmly on, there was little thought of football and the darkness of the songs to which I listened sound-tracked my life and emotions at that time. It was 'emo' music on repeat, songs that spoke of injustice, a lack of acceptance, and a clear motivation to escape one's current world for one of happiness and difference.

It is not hard to see why so many young people take their lives in Australia each year, fuelled by a grappling of identity and a desire to find some sense of belonging, in a world they see as nothing but judgemental and nasty.

My mind may have come to accept the sexual thoughts I had now admitted to, yet the transformation was far from complete. Seeking identity, I changed my look, grew my hair out, dyed it jet black and matched my fingernails with the same colour.

Black boots became my staple footwear and I began to wear ankle-length flowing skirts with long-sleeved cotton shirts. Most were black or purple and accessorised with beaded necklaces, rings and elaborate earrings. Home life became a living hell, with constant badgering and questions the norm. I could see the inevitable concern in my parents' eyes each and every time they saw me leave the house, as they asked themselves, "Is this just a normal teenage phase or is there something seriously wrong with our son?"

There were a few others like me in my area, such as a group of local girls determined to embrace a similar culture and ignite a revolution of change that they hoped to champion as they became older. We had met by chance at the local shopping centre, after one had commentated favourably on my skirt, assuming that I was in fact a female.

Despite being a little stunned at first, they seemed not to care one iota and became my core friendship group soon after. The boys I played football with were still in my thoughts, yet all bar Andrew had become too apprehensive to approach me, perhaps fearing some sort of social exclusion themselves or just plain afraid of the way I looked.

As a new football season approached, Andrew enquired about my potential involvement. For some reason I agreed to play, perhaps remembering the joy and escapism that the game had provided a few years earlier.

That decision was to prove a disaster.

Without competitive physical activity, my body had turned to mush. Once hard and supple, extra weight had appeared and my skin had taken on something of a pasty and white tone, after barely seeing the sun over the summer months.

I had begun wearing undersized sports bras and women's briefs, feeling freer than I ever had when out in public, and was shaving my legs weekly. Such decisions and my new 'look' were to cause a stir on the training ground when I walked the 100 metres or so across two football pitches from the bus stop on the adjacent main road.

I could hear a few giggles and murmurs as I approached, before total silence took over when I dumped my backpack near the group of assembling players and parents.

"Hi, everyone, it's nice to be back."

Other than Andrew warning his parents of my new 'style' and that warning being passed around amongst some of the others, I'm sure the majority of the boys would have had no idea who I was. What followed was the most awkward of silences and throughout the entire training session, the gay, cross-dressing left winger appeared to be the sole focus of the parents.

I heard most of their comments.

"What happened to him?"

"Is he still a boy?"

"This is confusing for the other boys."

The last was the most hurtful.

I could sense the eyes, the judgement, the attention, yet there was no escape that would do anything other than increase the focus of all three. I stayed for the entire session, played as hard as I could and left briskly in a flurry of tears, as soon as the coach's final thoughts were completed.

I sprinted across the fields towards the main road, was unable to face a group of kids around my age at the bus stop and walked the three kilometres home in an absolute mess. I was determined that once home, I would find a way to end everything.

I wanted to die.

A phone call as soon as I walked into my bedroom made me smile. It was Andrew.

"Hi, mate, are you okay? I thought you trained really well today."

We chatted for a few minutes before the details of a post training session vote were relayed to me by the one boy in the team who did not appear concerned by my appearance. The parents had voted almost unanimously that they would be taking their sons elsewhere should I be permitted to play in the team.

Apparently that message was solemnly delivered to my father later that night and in an Oscar-deserving performance, my off-handed dismissal of the news and insistence that I truly did not care ensured that the subject was dropped both immediately and for good.

In truth, it hurt. Yet in a strange way it was also liberating; it cut ties with a world to which I did not belong, was transitioning from and was determined to leave behind.

My girlfriends became the crutch keeping me upright. The bigots continued to rough me up at school. Mum and Dad hit the roof upon spotting female undergarments in the wash and without being completely aware of exactly what I was attempting to achieve, my transformation into a person who identified as a woman continued.

In unfamiliar surroundings, it felt like heaven. People speaking to me without any prior knowledge made for the most exhilarating sense of peace, yet there were always interactions in the school and local community to bring me back down to earth and serve as a reminder that to be truly free, I would need to be somewhere else and anonymous.

My father was a decent man. Not kind, warm or gentle, but decent in the sense that he worked hard and provided for a middle-class family living in a respectable suburb. That is the only positive thing I can say about him, the rest is best left unsaid.

By the time I entered the final two years of school and was living effectively as a woman, he had had enough. The school had rung with concerns and platitudes of support and family friends had begun visiting less frequently.

My father grew increasingly uncomfortable with the idea of his only son prancing around in a skirt and knickers and not pursuing a career in football, for which he had shown much aptitude.

When I stumbled across him in the garage one Sunday afternoon, sobbing and considerably drunk, everything finally came to a head. He stared straight at me and simply said, "You are a fucking faggot, pack your stuff and get out."

The following day I ceased attending school, packed my clothes in two large suitcases and stole $700 from my mother's bedside table.

Just three weeks earlier, one of the girls in my friendship group had relocated with her family to Sydney and after a teary phone call and the nod of approval from her parents, a northbound train was boarded that morning, with the distinct smell of freedom and future in the air.

Such a long journey presented ample opportunity to think. I pictured myself as Andy Dufresne from the movie *The Shawshank Redemption*—someone escaping a situation from which there appeared no clear path to do so. Rediscovering himself was Dufresne's motivation and doing so alone, a completely comfortable task to take on. However, like me, he had also made arrangements to catch up with an old friend.

Chloe had been the girl with whom I had shared the most throughout my transition. She understood me, had listened and advised where appropriate. Most importantly, she had never judged. Her father had invested in a pharmacy in Sydney, keen to escape the cold of Melbourne. Both he and his wife had been nothing but kind and supportive throughout my journey.

They took me in immediately, gave me employment in the family business and set me up in a small granny flat out the back. Chloe had informed them I was on my way and their welcome had made it feel like something of a homecoming.

That first night brought two divergent emotions: I felt the joy of knowing I was in a city where not a soul knew of my past, as well as the terror associated with ringing my mother and explaining exactly where I had disappeared to.

What I anticipated would be awkward and painful ended up being quite blunt and simple. She answered with a simple "Hello" before immediately interrupting when I began explaining the previous 24 hours.

She simply said, "Josh, I support your father on this. Leave us alone."

The line was cut immediately, as were the imperfect family relationships that had caused more harm than good throughout most of my life as a teenager.

With the natural fear of being in a new city and now effectively orphaned, sleep did not come easily for some weeks. However, with the confidence gained from employment, a safe place to stay and Chloe by my side, life eventually took on a new joy and positivity.

No one in Sydney looked twice as I frequented coffee shops, travelled on public transport, or served them diligently in the pharmacy. In truth, I felt beautiful as a woman and with the measured and supportive guidance of a local GP, began taking steps to embrace life as a female more fully.

Those two years as an adopted daughter were the best of my life to that point. Days were a simple existence of work, coffee, music, meals and sleep, yet in that simplicity there was also something so profound and empowering.

Yet there was one thing missing.

Now free of judgement, the notion of playing football again had begun nagging away consistently. Chloe too had played as a young girl. After turning 19 and signing the lease on a tiny one-bedroom unit just a kilometre or two from her family home, I took her for a coffee, with the intention of convincing her to join me as a member of a local women's team.

Chloe was apprehensive and concerned for my wellbeing, should anyone see or become aware of something that might trigger suspicion. However, when a mind is made up, it is often difficult to alter and the best thing for a concerned friend to potentially do is go along for the ride.

That is exactly what Chloe did.

Throughout that summer, we whet our appetites for the upcoming winter season by frequenting Sydney FC and Western Sydney Wanderers women's matches. The speed of the play was impressive, especially seated at close quarters, and my eyes were constantly drawn to the wider players, particularly on the left, as they sought to make space and fire balls into the box for the strikers to latch on to.

The reconnection with football at those matches brought me to tears on more than one occasion. I missed the game immensely and often sat with moist eyes, as Chloe placed her arm around me in support. The ice was often broken by her insistence that I would "kill it" playing against naturally born women, yet tumbling testosterone levels would ensure a playing field far more level than the one she was expecting to witness.

Visiting a sports store to purchase a pair of football boots brought back cherished childhood memories of pre-season preparations. Doing so with Chloe only made things more complete and by the time we pulled into the car park adjoining a suburban synthetic pitch on a warm late February evening, my anticipation was at an immeasurable high.

As other players gathered and a few stretches and kick-ups began, there seemed to be a wonderful sense of community present.

It was simply inspiring; they were passionate footballers who were there to play, unconcerned by the back story of who they were playing with.

Within weeks, I had never felt so supported and happy in my entire life. I was home.

Actually, Chloe and I were lucky to even make it home that first evening. When made aware of the traditional piss-up that followed the first training session of the season, we had assumed it would be something of a conservative affair, designed to encourage relationships and bonding within the group. Instead, it became a rather wild and unforgettable night.

A local establishment dished up gourmet pizzas, the drinks flowed and by the time three members of the team were shoeless and dancing on an outdoor table in the warm summer air, I knew we were in trouble.

I can vaguely recall chatting with each and every member of the team in what the coach Rebecca referred to as "speed dating football". It was a brilliant idea and the stories we shared reflected the poetry and integrity in all of our lives, no matter from whence we came or the journey undertaken to arrive at the club.

Not a player enquired about my gender, sexuality, nor preferences. They cared little and appeared more interested in where I could best contribute on the pitch. I was still yet to engage in a physical relationship with a man and being surrounded by so many magnificently attractive and stimulating women had me unsure as to exactly where my future would lie in terms of romantic love.

However, on that night, none of it mattered, and when a stunningly beautiful central defender named Trish announced to the group that my left foot and attacking skills would fill a gaping hole on the left-hand side, I accepted the role.

Just six months earlier, a woman named Jennifer had passed after a brave fight with breast cancer. She had been the long-standing left-sided attacker in the team, a mum of three and a primary school teacher by day. A few tears were shed during the subsequent discussion around her death and importance to the team, as the details of the tragedy were conveyed movingly to the new additions.

Trish was quite pissed at the time and leaped onto her chair to announce to the group that their mate's legacy was to be honoured and continued by me, Juliette. She stumbled through a sentence that went something like, "We'll always miss our Jen, but this little chickadee has been sent to replace her,

WHEN MUM AND DAD SEE ME KICK

we are so fucking lucky."

From that day on, my nickname amongst the team was 'Lucky'.

I'd never had a nickname before and felt chuffed that the group had blessed me with one so quickly. Chloe was less pleased with her new moniker of 'chucker' after a few too many cocktails had seen her visit the bathroom for a quick vomit somewhere around 10 p.m.

In time, she would grow to see the sense of belonging those nicknames fostered. However, there were also some weird ones that I never really got to the bottom of. Shelly was labelled 'Supermum' after popping out five kids with husband Gareth. Helen was known only as 'Nana Mouskouri', with her Greek heritage a giveaway as to why. Our 44-year-old goalkeeper Gwen was known only as 'Canteen', a place she was found on weekdays at her kids' primary school.

One nickname I never really grasped was the one given to our star striker Janice; a seriously gifted athlete, she was simply known as 'the Dildo'. Despite feeling motivated to do so on many occasions, I never quite summoned the strength to ask of its origin. I guess if there was anyone on the planet understanding of the need for some things to simply remain unsaid, it was me. I applied that to Janice's rather saucy nickname and just enjoyed watching her play football instead.

Six weeks later, as I stood on the left touchline and waited for the first kick-off of the season to take place, my heart raced. I was now free, a woman, employed, loved and about to kick a competitive football for the first time in years.

At first, I decided to hold back a little, naively thinking that my genetics might indeed give me something of an advantage. Within minutes, the quality of the players around me and the toughness of the contest threw such thoughts out the proverbial window and I was into the fray as fiercely as the rest.

After ten minutes, Chloe slipped a lovely pass between a central defender and the opposition's right back. I ducked in behind, collected the pass and chipped the ball to the far post where 'the Dildo' headed home from close range.

An artist capable of painting a picture of my heart at that moment would have constructed the most beautiful artwork imaginable. It felt like I'd come full circle.

That team and those women were to become my life.

To this day, I still do not know what the members of the team know or have discovered about my past. Chloe certainly never unlocked the vault, of that I am certain. Who knows, I may well have even broken a few by-laws by playing as a woman all these years, especially if my circumstances were to be considered alongside some of the recent legal disputes involving transgender athletes around the globe.

Yet in a way it makes little difference to me or the beautiful queens with whom I play. We are all over 30 now; some players have come and gone and a core group are strapping up for another season to be played on ageing legs and with enthusiastic hearts.

There may well be hundreds of women with whom I have played and competed against that are completely unaware that I was actually born a Joshua and later became a Juliette. Perhaps the odd player would cry foul, yet something tells me that the majority would instead cite the beauty of the game and its ability to invite all to be embraced in its welcoming arms.

Along with Chloe, it probably saved my life.

GRAHAM,
AGE 52

For most kids, the thought of being the last player selected by two respected captains in schoolyard play is about as humiliating as it gets.

However, for me, that was commonplace and something with which I became used to throughout my entire school life. It wasn't due to any hatred or disrespect from those charged with selecting the players they needed to earn bragging rights during that particular lunchtime game, more just because I was pretty useless when it came to sport.

Tucked away on a high shelf in my walk-in at home is a small box with all the awards and commendations I received at school. There are a number of merit certificates, a bizarre medal celebrating my participation in something called a Computer Marathon and a few debating prizes that came my way in secondary school.

Yet there is not one single item, award, certificate or medal based on sporting prowess, achievement or even participation.

It is fairly easy to sit back and have a chuckle about that state of affairs now, with little bitterness or regret and a blunt realisation that I was simply uncoordinated and useless on a sporting field.

However, that never stopped me from having a go and despite my parents probably turning their heads in sheer embarrassment and/or hilarity whilst watching me compete, they certainly gave me every chance to succeed.

As a skinny, short and lightweight kid growing up in Adelaide in the late 1970s, Australian Rules football was naturally the first cab off the rank. I struggled. For some reason, whenever the ball miraculously landed in my hands, I froze.

As if rooted to the spot and without any concept of the rules or point of the game, I became cannon fodder for other kids looking to apply a powerful tackle. Time after time I was lifted off my feet by aggressive and bigger kids who lapped up the roars of the mums and dads cheering from the sideline.

Every now and then I would limp off the field in tears, frustrated and disappointed as the game carried on without me.

Thankfully, my parents eventually saw the light and after two years of what must have been agony for them, as the owners of the little useless kid who always lessened the chances of the team whenever he took to the field, other sporting possibilities were pursued.

I took tennis lessons for six months, faring little better, yet suffering far less physical punishment. The day I lingered around the coach's small office at the local tennis complex and heard him say, "He doesn't have much of a serve, his backhand is awful and I am struggling to control his forehand, but he is doing pretty well," I knew two things.

Firstly, that the coach was a mighty good salesman and secondly, that Mum and Dad were getting ripped off! Tennis was not to be my thing.

Perhaps standing out in the hot Australian summer sun would bring more luck. At nine, I joined a local cricket club and set about learning the rules and intricacies of a game that still confuses me to this very day.

My cricketing achievements could best be described as twofold. I always provided my teammates with a laugh and became adept at packing up the kit at the completion of Thursday night training sessions.

Each week, players padded up with all the necessary protective equipment, patiently waiting for their five minutes of batting practice in the nets. I loathed the thought of it and within minutes was usually struck in the testicles by a thunderbolt from one of the talented bowlers we had.

As I writhed around on the ground, the coach and remainder of the team would chuckle as they sportingly enquired as to my welfare. It is one of the quirky nuances in the game. There is nothing funnier to male cricketers than seeing someone struck somewhere between the belly button and the knee, despite all being fully aware of just how much it hurts.

It is likely that the quiet smirks and laughter are actually something of a silent cricketing prayer, spoken by players sincerely thankful that they were not the victim.

Head injury assessments have become commonplace in modern sport, with

WHEN MUM AND DAD SEE ME KICK

protection of the head a serious issue. My cricket career necessitated a groin injury assessment protocol, so frequently was I doubled up in the nets and gasping for breath.

In true fighting spirit, the cricket experiment also lasted two seasons and I can distinctly recall never taking a catch or completing a run out, and scoring a grand total of seven runs. The entire seven were accumulated via unintentional edges and mis-hits that would be superb GIFs if the technology to create them had been around at the time.

Next up was basketball, another unmitigated failure, and then what we at the time referred to as soccer.

I recall a conversation between my father and I, where he expressed a view that the round ball game might be the one for me. His thinking was that the skills required to merely participate were of the most basic variety and that surely I could be shoved in defence somewhere to plug a gap or simply hoof the ball out of danger when required.

That line of thinking appeared to be shared by the coach, who used me in that role for the entire season I played the game. Sadly for him, rather than being an effective plug in defence, I was more of a leaky pipe that allowed skilful and talented players far too much space.

When I attempted to clear the ball it travelled only short distances and without the speed to match zippy attackers, they simply whizzed by me with ease. I was useless as a player, yet did fall in love with the game.

It was the first time in my sporting life that, despite the zero talent I possessed in the endeavour, a game had actually made me feel keen to come back the following week and do it all over again. Some might wonder why, considering I too heard the moans and sighs from the sideline whenever a player made me look very, very silly in defence. However, the overall success of the team somehow negated my personal failings.

Put simply, we were a very good team, thanks mainly to two boys named Josh who scored goal after goal for us in the under 12s competition.

Sure, every now and then I was made to look a goose and hang my head as another goal dribbled into our net, yet for every time we conceded, the Joshes would score twice. When they did, I enjoyed the chance to run towards them and jump on their backs and the team went bananas at least a few times every Saturday morning.

Despite knowing that I had contributed little, the goal celebrations made me feel a part of something and for a kid who had never managed to earn that right before, filled a void that subsequently felt great.

The game became something of an obsession. I soaked up as much of it as I could on television and even managed to convince Dad to take me to a few NSL games featuring Adelaide City. I continued to try my best, probably improved a little and felt less embarrassed the longer the season went, yet was still by far the least talented player in the team.

Then a moment that changed my life took place at a school assembly in 1983.

An official from the local football association spoke at our weekly sports assembly, encouraging kids to become involved in the game if they were not already so and enquiring as to whether any young players might be interested in becoming referees.

Something twigged in my head immediately.

As a debater, I had always been confident speaking and expressing clear ideas. Not intimidated by the task of addressing others and commanding a situation, I wondered whether those skills might perhaps cross over into the world of officiating sport.

I took a flyer from the speaker and pursued the possibility in secret for a week or two, before eventually broaching the subject with my parents. To my surprise, they lit up light beacons, also seeing the potential merit in the idea.

I sensed in them a hopeful joy that their clumsy son may have finally found a pathway to long-term participation in a sport that he was so passionate about.

These days, the process of becoming a football referee has layers of complication that did not exist back at that time. After submitting the appropriate paperwork, I was encouraged to attain a copy of FIFA's official rule book, purchase a good-quality whistle and be measured up for a referee's uniform.

There was little delay, with football a growing sport right around the country and a dearth of referees to cover the increasing popularity of the game.

Initially, I tagged along with a senior official, learning the basics, before spending a great deal of time learning the role of the referee's assistant. There was a clear focus on the importance of assessing the precise position of players when it came to off-side decisions.

When informed that I had picked up the skill as quickly as any young referee that my mentor had seen, I felt sure that my decision to enter the world of refereeing was a correct one. I completed the training courses required as quickly as possible, with the idea of officiating an actual game the carrot to doing so.

As a young teenager, I took full control of a match for the first time. In little more than six months, the powers at be had deemed me competent enough to oversee an under 6s game, featuring a host of players who reminded me a lot of myself when it came to football talent.

Frankly, there was not a lot to do, with the ball ping-ponging around a small area in the centre of the pitch and rarely finding its way into open space. There were few tackles, the odd tear after balls cannoned into kids from very close range and sadly, no goals.

Most compelling was the manner in which the players all listened intently to whatever I said. That was something, outside of debating competitions, which I had never experienced before. Frankly, I enjoyed the feelings of authority and control.

The best piece of advice I ever received came from someone who would these days be described as a referee development officer. After explaining how enjoyable it was to have control of the game and feel confident and authoritative whilst refereeing, my mentor spoke with wisdom and clarity after the game.

"Graham, whilst it is good to have control and be the boss when out on the pitch, just remember, the parents are not there to watch you.

"Your job is to manage the game as invisibly as you can and create an environment that allows an excellent game of football to take place.

"Your interaction with the players dictates that. If you are firm, consistent and precise, they will not waste their time testing you out. If you are wishy-washy and weak, they will have you running in circles in quick time."

Whilst undoubtedly not a word-for-word recount of the discussion, I took what is essentially a three-step checklist on board and applied it throughout what became a long and enjoyable career as a referee.

In essence, my three principles became:

1/ I am not the centre of attention

2/ Create an environment that encourages good football

3/ Be decisive and clear!

I am fairly sure that many of the men and women officiating the game at the elite level may have never considered, or simply forgotten, one or more of these principles. Watching referees perform rather dramatically, emotionally and self-consciously when in charge of matches always makes me cringe.

As does a whistle-blower who effectively ruins the entire contest by an either over or under-application of the rules, therefore hampering the ability of the teams to play an attractive brand of football.

Seeing referees surrounded by hordes of players applying psychological pressure after a contentious decision is particularly disturbing, with weakness sensed and control lost thanks to error or a rather unconvincing enforcement of the rules.

The best referees are usually quite passive in their presence, responsible for quality matches where the action is allowed to flow and direct enough with players to discourage the questioning of decisions. There is little point taking up an issue with a referee if a player has had dealings with them before and is quite sure that nothing they say will alter a decision, nor gain them some advantage in the future.

In saying that, it was not as though I always got things right on the pitch.

Perhaps a little over-confident after a couple of seasons controlling competitive matches, a low-level semi-final in the under 11s age group came my way and a cracking game of football played out between two evenly matched teams.

With around three minutes left on my timepiece and the scores locked at 2–2, a throw was won by the team applying all the late pressure and in excellent field position, a late winner did seem on the cards.

Unfortunately, with parents shouting and cheering from the sidelines, a hurricane-like breeze whistling across the park and my fuel tank close to empty after two earlier matches, I made a significant blunder.

As the ball crossed the sideline and with the attacking team keen to take the throw quickly, I extended my arm incorrectly and awarded it to the wrong team. The seconds that followed were a blur. As the rightful winners of the throw stood in disbelief the moment my arm was raised, their opponents, to their credit, grabbed the ball and returned it to play, streaming upfield in the process.

My brain strongly suggested that I blow the whistle and call back the play, yet in the three or four seconds it took to register the error and the possible solution, it appeared to be too late. I followed the play downfield as the team in wrongful possession approached the attacking box and played a lovely angled ball to their right-winger.

He cut back inside, beat two players and fired from around 15 metres, finding the keeper's net in the top right corner.

As the goal scorer went mental and was tackled and mauled by teammates, the parents of the jilted team let rip. I heard every word, every curse and nothing else, as I signalled the goal and returned to the centre of the pitch to recommence the match.

I was 15 at the time and when a burly voice shouted, "You wait, ref, you just wait," I truly understood what the phrase 'fear of God' meant. I trembled through the final minute or so of the match, hoping there would be an equaliser, even adding on a few seconds to try and make it happen, but it didn't.

As both sides gathered on their respective sides of halfway, one celebrating and the other receiving pats on the back of encouragement, I walked a slow trudge to my bag on the side of the pitch, within metres of the team that I had potentially just robbed of a grand final.

The coach and parents spoke to their boys indirectly, lacing every word with anger towards me.

"Don't worry, boys, you played great. If we had a proper referee things might have turned out differently."

"Well played Rovers, one stupid decision by a blind idiot cost you the game. We'll make a formal complaint."

"Idiot bloody referee needs to get his eyes checked. What a dickhead."

On reflection, there is probably a little bit of truth in each of the above comments. I had indeed made an awful error, potentially robbed the team finishing the most strongly of the two, and it was hard not to disagree with those on the sideline and their views on the reliability of my eyesight.

There were a few quiet tears shed that evening, especially after a senior official had spoken to me in the immediate aftermath of the event. Too scared to admit openly to the error, I lied, claiming that I thought that the ball had last touched the opposite team to which it actually had.

The official clarified that recollection of events a couple of times and simply said, "Well done, lad, if that is what you saw, that should be your decision. Wrong or right, you did the right thing."

Not only was I a shit referee, I had quickly become a shit and corrupt referee! The shame I felt was immense and it took months to begin to see the innocence within which the decision was made and to stop beating myself up for what was an honest mistake.

Looking back now, it is clear that the key issue was not so much the error itself, a mistake referees all around the world make from time to time, it was more the lack of confidence to correct it immediately. No doubt, if I had simply blown the whistle as the eventual winners took off downfield with the ball, perhaps saying, "Sorry, boys, I've got that one wrong," the situation would have simmered within seconds and the game continued.

However, as a teenager without the confidence to do so and concerned that any admission of error would create a perception of weakness, I had simply frozen under pressure.

Thankfully, we either win or learn in life and any future decisions that required a quick adjustment or alteration, as few and far between as they may have been, were handled briskly and with an apologetic confidence. It took just one awful experience and a heck of a lot of reflection to realise that it is far more important to get a decision right than be too concerned by what others might think about your competency.

In fact, being open to admit to error and happy to adjust for the sake of accuracy can actually enhance people's perception of officials. At least, that has been my experience.

Refereeing football matches became pretty much all I thought about through secondary school. By 17 and struggling with every subject on the curriculum, weekends were spent at local parks as textbooks remained firmly closed on my bookshelf.

At the time, school success, or a lack of it, meant little to me. A busy weekend refereeing could see an earn of around $50–$60, a tidy sum during the 1980s, when a packet of hot chips and a can of soft drink would set you back just a couple of dollars.

Summer soccer also grew in popularity, which saw weeknight matches played in the warmer months, as players sought to improve fitness levels for the upcoming winter season.

It was those hot and exhausting nights that coincided with my promotion to senior matches and I would be lying to suggest that I was not a little nervous about officiating with players far older than me participating.

Frankly, it was a real eye-opener. No matter how talented some players had been at junior level, there was usually a parent or guardian nearby and I saw very few incidents of bad sportsmanship across the four seasons where I worked exclusively with junior players.

There was the odd player who had called me fuckwit, or retard, or arsehole—all shown yellow cards, by the way—and a few physical stoushes between players requiring separation, yet mostly, there were very few issues.

That all changed dramatically when I began officiating senior matches in the late 1980s.

I saw a central defender head-butt an opponent, knocking him out cold in the opening minutes of a night match, had one fixture turn into an all-in brawl by half-time and was responsible for the sending off of a player who was subsequently banned from football for life.

I'm not too sure what was exactly wrong with the player who the state federation saw as having no place in the game in South Australia. He spat in my general direction as we gathered on the pitch ready for kick-off, talked trash to his opponents from the moment the opening whistle sounded, and picked a fight with a much smaller and younger player midway through the second half.

When the gutsy little winger decided to stand up for himself, the bully sprinted to the sideline where a pile of builders' rubble had been dumped and returned, brick in hand, chasing his opponent in a mad rage.

He nabbed his target about 30 metres behind the goal at the opposite end of the pitch to which the play continued and began to smash the brick into the temple of his victim. Players from both teams sprinted to his aid, yet being more than 100 metres away from the incident, it took a good 15 or so seconds for anyone to arrive.

To their credit, his teammates tore the oaf from the younger man and pinned him to the ground amidst shouts and mayhem. I blew my whistle and to this very day often ask myself why.

The game was instantly abandoned, as an ambulance was called for the victim. Unconscious and blood across much of his face, it was the most astonishing and concerning sight I have ever witnessed on a football pitch and something I hope never to see again.

Thankfully, most matches played out without incident, yet the step up to senior level refereeing tested the principles by which I stood and it was a real pleasure to hop back into junior ranks every now and again.

Not all memories from those formative years are as alarming or concerning. Plenty are mighty funny and if I ever find the time, there could well be a book in the stories I've gathered.

I'll never forget a young boy named Gareth who arrived at his weekly under 8s football match with a bad case of gastroenteritis and lost the contents of his bowels on the edge of his defensive box and right across the back of his freshly washed and splendidly white pair of shorts.

There was an under 12s player who, whilst defending, turned towards his own net and thumped home what he thought was a stunning shot at a decisive moment in the match. I'll never forget the overheard words of his mother on the sideline, who simply said, "Oh my God, that is my son … how embarrassing."

Considering my own failures on football pitches whilst playing the game, I knew exactly how both parent and player felt.

There were plenty of broken noses, tears, blows taken to the groin region and wild weather conditions, that sometimes created the most comical of football matches.

During an under 7s game, the ball never once passed halfway throughout the entire first half, thanks to a ferocious wind that literally knocked a player or two off their feet. The team running with the aid of the wind led 5–0 at the break and when the teams changed ends for the second half, the unthinkable happened.

Once again, the ball never crossed halfway and the team in deficit racked up five goals of their own to earn a point, in what was a ripping drawn match played on half a football pitch.

I saw the goalkeeper from the non-active end walk off the pitch, approach his parents and say out loud, "That was sooooo boring." Sometimes football can be that way.

One specific challenge for which I felt ready was officiating women's matches. As the game continued to call more and more female players in Australia during the 1990s, playing venues, facilities and referee supplies became more and more stretched and valuable.

I had encountered many a cheeky player over the years and handled most with a firm hand and a respectful tone, yet wondered how different things would be when in control of a women's game. I knew the basic differences between men and women, you know, the biological stuff, but had no idea as to what to expect in terms of banter, swearing, attitude and aggression.

In reality, there was very little difference, with f-bombs as common as in the men's game, the aggression and competitiveness high, and players just as likely to disagree and become irate with decisions.

However, there was one female team in north Adelaide that did unsettle me each and every time I was rostered to officiate its matches. It was a long relationship that began on a blowy Sunday morning with the goals flowing.

Stuck in defence and struggling to contain an opposition scoreline that was already into double digits, the team in red took up their defensive positions as a free-kick on the edge of the box was planned.

Two women just to my right began a conversation.

"Jen, how many goals have they scored?"

"Eleven, I think."

"Shit, that's not good. Can we just finish the game now and go to the pub, ref?"

I ignored her. She continued.

"Hey, ref, c'mon. Blow the whistle. There can't be too long to go!"

Again, I ignored her.

"C'mon, ref. Blow full-time after this free-kick and you can do whatever you want to me!"

The free-kick was taken and the match continued with the player in question pursuing me up the field.

"I think you are hot, ref! Will you go out with me?"

It was at this point I realised that the woman in question was either visually impaired or completely taking the mickey, with the second option appearing to be the most likely.

I responded, "I'd love to, but I'm busy for the next four years."

"Damn," she replied.

As I blew the final whistle to end the match shortly after, she approached me, offered her hand in gratitude for my efforts and said rather seductively, "We could have been something special, hottie."

She had me in the palm of her hand and each and every time I took to the pitch to referee one of her team's matches, she would throw me a wink, a look and telepathically let me know that a kind refereeing performance was expected.

I tried to be impartial, as always, yet wonder in retrospect whether that young woman played me for a fool and had me completely hoodwinked in the process.

Did I dish out the cards and award the free-kicks to her opponents at the same rate I did to her team? I'd like to think so. Yet every time I ran on the pitch with that saucy number four leering in my direction, I must admit to being somewhat distracted.

By the time the 21st century rolled around, I'd been refereeing for around 16 years and been lucky enough to graduate to high-quality matches in the state league. There, I saw some marvellous players and met some marvellous people.

The stakes were always high, the players well versed in how to 'play' a referee as best they could, and the families, friends and fans in the stands open and unfiltered in their advice and criticism.

Mostly, as an experienced referee, such criticism had become like water off the proverbial duck's back, yet one day in the heat of a March pre-season match in west Adelaide, I felt true fear for only the second time as an official.

Despite no points being on the table, two sides with a long history and an obvious ethnic tension between them went hammer and tong, seemingly intent to inflict body count damage that would hamper each other's preparations for the upcoming season.

It was brutal from the opening whistle and I recall dishing out five or six cards in the first 15 minutes in an attempt to get the game back under control.

Sadly, I was simply not good enough to do so, with neither side relaxing their physical assaults on the opposition, and the match quickly slipped from my grasp. After half an hour of play, an aggressive midfielder dove studs up and feet first into an opposition defender, sending him face over apex into the turf.

Players ran from all directions, with the melee set to begin and me standing in the middle of 20-odd men with fire in their eyes. I blew the whistle as loudly as possible, wedged myself in between the two combatants and did all I could to keep the peace.

In effect, there was no point, with both sides having turned up for the match with the intent to fight and win, with my peace-keeper role not ever standing a chance.

I stepped away as the tension inflamed and fists, feet and foreheads flew, in a brief brawl that only ended when the benches were cleared. The cooler heads held back the men enraptured by violence and those firmly engaged in the heat of battle.

With something of a peace restored, the need for action was obvious.

I ushered the two teams into their respective sides of the pitch and dished out four yellow cards to men who had charged into battle with no real reason to do so. Then, I called over the instigator and showed him a straight red.

Oddly, he did nothing. He simply stood and glared at me as though I had just murdered his entire family.

Then, in a flurry of movement, his right arm cocked and flew in the direction of my left temple. Thankfully, my reactions were on point and I evaded the swinging arm, before his left knee was lifted towards my groin and I fended it away with my card-holding hand.

The whole incident occurred in a blur and thankfully some level-headed teammates had the player restrained and proceeded to frogmarch him to the sideline. There, he was chaperoned into the sheds and not to be seen again for the remainder of what continued to be a tense and nasty match.

When the 90 minutes were done and the players and supporters had mostly departed the stadium, I walked slowly to my car after making a few phone calls in the referees' room. Just a few vehicles remained and after throwing my bag into the boot, I reached to open my driver's side door, only to be confronted by the man I had sent from the pitch an hour or so earlier.

"Hey, cunt, not so fuckin' tough now, are you?"

To this day I am not sure how anyone should respond to the above sentence, yet in true debating style, I attempted to negotiate.

I laid out my case. "Look, mate, I know you are upset, but any referee would have sent you off for that tackle. It was dangerous and you know it."

Sadly, the mind of the man wanting to tear me to pieces was not particularly interested in negotiation.

"Don't give me your ref bullshit, you're a dumb fuck fag and I'm gonna knock your fuckin' head off."

Seemingly boxed into a corner where physical confrontation was inevitable, I tried an old debating trick.

"Okay, mate, what would you do if someone slid in the way you did?" If anything, it bought me a few precious seconds.

He replied, "What the fuck do you mean?"

Sensing a chance to avoid a bashing, I said, "Well, if someone from the other team had tackled you like that, what would you want me to do?"

"Well, you should send them off!"

The idiot was well within the range of the net with just a final flourish required. "Exactly, mate, and that is what I did to you. It doesn't matter which team you play for, I just call it as I see it and you were out of line today."

He flustered a little more. "But you are a filthy referee cunt."

I responded just as two club officials drifted into sight to check that all vehicles had departed the car park. "No, I'm not, mate; I'm a father with a couple of kids, a decent bloke and someone who was so shit at football that he decided to become a referee!"

"Is everything alright here, men?" enquired the club president as he approached his wildest player and the referee who had just sent him from the field.

I replied, "Yep, all fine here, boss, just having a chat with an old mate and explaining my decision today. I think we are all good now."

The president shot me a look of understanding and I noted that the player departed the club soon after, never to grace a match I controlled again.

It might sound like something of a wild ride, yet as I enter my 40th year of football officialdom, it strikes me that the number of great people, fantastic players and supportive parents far outweigh the nut-jobs encountered along the way.

Sadly, my physical abilities were to ensure that playing the game at a high level was categorically out of the question. Whilst that could have resulted in some football bitterness and perhaps a complete rejection of the game, refereeing provided a peripheral avenue to be involved in what is the most beautiful sport on the planet.

Mostly, it was smooth sailing, bar a shocking throw-in decision, a brick-brandishing thug, some loose football bowels and a crazed maniac seeking to kill me in a car park. It was fortunate that I always had my three principles on board and some debating prowess to get me out of a scrap or two along the way.

I would guess that most successful referees have a bag of tricks just like mine.

STUART,
AGE 48

I grew up in a bloody quiet house. So quiet in fact that wooden spoons could be heard gently stirring pots on the stove top from rooms away.

It was by design and on demand. An intense and rather intimidating father ensured that things remained calm, composed and to his liking whenever he was in the home. There were rare moments to bust out of the silence and parental trips to supermarkets and fruit shops provided them.

Music volumes were ramped up to the absurd whenever such rare moments presented themselves. The only sounds louder than the songs being played were the screaming voices of two young people regularly denied the basic and most liberating freedom of singing along to the most modern of music.

I am the younger of two siblings and my energies were funnelled even more passionately to music than my sister's, despite her obvious talent on a keyboard and love of 1980s pop. So much so, that after dinner had been consumed on pleasant evenings and a hasty retreat from the table requested, I walked to a local park some half a kilometre from the family home.

It was a vast expanse, with four cricket pitches laid out equidistantly. One picket-fenced main oval with a grandstand capable of holding around 1,000 people overlooked the entire scene. Desperate to flee the home and its feelings of restriction, I would head to the pitch located most centrally and check that the park was devoid of anyone in close enough proximity to eavesdrop on what was still a somewhat shy and nervous boy attempting to find his voice.

Essentially, I would scream. The lyrics left my mouth with full venom as I stretched and strained to hit some of the more difficult notes. I knew I could sing a little, stay in key and hold a decent melody. However, the agility achieved in those sessions developed my voice at a rapid rate.

Within months I was confident and competent, yet still kept what is one of the most satisfying times in my life hidden from the other members of the household. In fact, the odd barb continued to be thrown my way at family gatherings, as my mother would comically inform relatives of the lack of singing ability in the family and the fact that I was, in her view, tone deaf.

Years later, the penny dropped for her. I played in a few bands, made regular appearances at the church where my children attended primary school and wrote songs for friends, colleagues and most importantly, my wife.

I was no Bruce Springsteen, but I loved the free expression of music and the power of it, something no doubt born from the quiet and overbearing house in which I grew up.

The ongoing tone of apprehension at number 63 was not really explained until many years later, when my father announced that he was becoming ill with Huntington's Disease. One younger brother and two older sisters of his had also inherited the gene that makes for a quality of life that slowly declines over time, as involuntary movements and physiological torment take over.

It is truly an awful disease, with one clear symptom being a difficulty in coping when multiple or excessive sounds are made in close proximity to a sufferer. Hence the family home and the rather eerie reality of it.

With the next generation of relatives now also afflicted by Huntington's and suffering around me, music remains a hideaway and the place that when travelled to, provides a sense of peace and isolation, and removes all the awful realities of a horrific disease.

However, singing wasn't the only thing I kept secret as a young boy.

In the 1970s, the Canterbury-Bankstown district in Sydney was a migrant hub. Families of Australia's first significant wave of economic migrants in the 1950s had now become a second generation.

Football lay at the centre of many of those communities and sporting clubs offered emotional and collective support for people struggling with the expected language and cultural challenges prevalent in migrant groups.

The galvanising effect created by the establishment of such clubs drew little support from the wider Australian community. Most felt threatened, many insulted and to this day, the odd red-necked hillbilly still rears their head in

Australian society when commenting on the round-ball game.

It seems rather sad to me that in 2023, we still hear racist and discriminatory views about people who did little more than seek a better life in a safer country.

The issue was raised frequently in my childhood home through the 1970s and 80s. Women wearing headwear were referred to as 'scarves', anyone of Asian appearance was openly described as a second-class citizen and I remember a specific joke about the garlic breath of a certain Italian educator during a parent-teacher interview.

There were also constant references to Aboriginal athletes going 'walk-about' during competition and the use of common Indigenous slurs that I refuse to give the dignity of print.

The day my mother instructed me to never partake in a doner kebab as "you never know who the donor is" pretty much sums up the rather narrow-minded worldview that was presented to me as a child, with a disrespect for football a natural extension of it.

Images on television of those so-called crazy Italians, mad Greeks and loony Croatians engaging in tense and sometimes violent conduct at National Soccer League matches were frequently the centrepiece of dining room conversation, especially when my parents could see the growing interest that I had in kicking a sphere around their quarter-acre block.

Frankly, I was getting pretty good at it, able to shape a ball, time a volley and now playing one-on-ones with friends most afternoons.

No doubt, those dinner conversations were a flawed attempt to divert my attention away from football by talking about the potential harm they foresaw in it, and a clear effort to keep me participating in the more culturally accepted endeavours in which I had competed since the age of five.

Stereotypical commentary from my immediate and extended family reinforced my parents' view of football as something of an emasculating and embarrassing exercise played by weak European men. As a captive and subservient nine-year-old, it was tough to dissent and the desperation they all showed in steering me away from the beautiful game would be a therapist's dream today.

Modern-day psychologists would be intrigued with the degree of emotional bullying undertaken, based on the most fragile of complexes possessed by my kin. In truth, they were a collection of drunkards, abusers and fools, possessing a level of intelligence that even as a small boy, made me question what the true definition of an adult should be.

All the while, I kept singing and slowly became aware of the most hypocritical of ironies.

Despite constant mockery around and the assault on Australian football, the current English champions often got a mention at family gatherings. Half-pissed men puffed their chests out and claimed knowledge about the game that even a small boy could identify as fraudulent.

Typical Liverpool allegiances were common, jumping onto a winner is something Australian bandwagoners are traditionally good at, and the odd Tottenham Hotspur gag was made.

I can still vividly remember chomping away on my grandmother's appallingly flavoured and presented salmon patties, listening to the ill-informed shit sprouted by my relatives and thinking, "If anyone says anything bad about my Hammers I will leap across this table and punch them in the nose."

But the secret needed to remain kept and no one was to know just how much I loved that club, looking up their results secretly in newspapers as soon as they hit the coffee table, nor the ever-present desire I had to play the game in a formal setting.

Rather clumsily, my father had always sat up late to watch highlights of the top-flight of English football. More clumsily, he had let me do the same, beginning sometime in the late 1970s. Surely his concerns around my involvement in the Australian game would only increase by permitting a weekly dose of football that could potentially lead to a love affair with the game?

Despite something of a limited and juvenile understanding of football at the time, what I witnessed in those hourly highlight packages inspired me and they always seemed to be over in a flash, almost before they had even begun.

After watching each edition and hearing my father grunt and groan after a stunning goal or impressive save, I wondered why a man so apparently intent on hating the Australian game and forbidding his son to attend matches or participate in them would be so interested in watching English football religiously, on delay, from thousands of kilometres away.

As is often the case with young children, West Ham was his team and thus mine. The broadcast was never more compelling than in the few moments where the claret and blue appeared. Without the modern luxuries of cable television and depending on the number of goals scored during the Hammers' fixture, the East London club's appearance could be as brief as a minute and scarcely longer than three.

In the early to mid-1980s, they were minutes I looked forward to like no others.

Of course, I kept those emotions in check and showed little, knowing that too much football passion might well see me sent to bed before the completion of the program, with hidden tears the result.

My earliest memories of watching football entail grasping a warm mug of hot chocolate on FA Cup Final night, with legs tucked up on the lounge as winter approached, marvelling at the skill of the players and being all too scared to exclaim anything at all.

During the weekly highlights, I longed to shout out support for Billy Bonds, Trevor Brooking and Frank Lampard, yet knew that such a move would dangerously fill the cone of silence that my father's illness demanded.

To this day, I do not know whether it was his disease or insistence that football in Australia was so inherently flawed and culturally vacuous that most fuelled my fear of expressing a passion towards it. I'll probably never know which was the strongest factor in keeping me hush and often hope that it was illness more than narrowmindedness, yet I cannot be sure.

As such, highlights package after highlights package, FA Cup Final after FA Cup Final, I bit my tongue through sheer fear, falling ever more in love with the game.

Rather embarrassingly, I still have vivid memories of using the garden hose to water the square pitch I had defined in the backyard. I would soak the surface to a point at which I was content it reflected an English pitch on a wet day. (Please note that such actions were undertaken well and truly before strict water restrictions began being enforced by state authorities.)

Once drenched, the Hammers took to the field to take on Liverpool in a 90-minute contest that, strangely, the claret and blue won each and every time. Sorry, Reds, you may have won the title on many occasions, but you could never beat West Ham United in the Thomas' back yard. We had your measure every single day.

Somehow, I played out those contests alone, without even a friend or my sister willing to participate. Those 'matches' are potentially the reason behind the craving for community that has motivated so many of my life decisions. I felt lonely, sometimes still do, and really just wanted somebody to talk to.

As I entered my teenage years, football continued to intrigue me. After the migration of the 70s, my 1980s school yearbook reflected a multicultural melting pot. From a standard class of 30, the mix looked something like this—ten or so Anglos, three or four Asians, five to six Lebanese or Middle Eastern boys and a hodgepodge in the other third, including Italians, Greeks, Brazilians, Filipinos and what was then, Yugoslavs.

There was even an Irish lad named Brendan Burns who towelled me up on the asphalt playground time after time. He frustrated the heck out of me by refusing to take a touch and merely turning onto the path of the ball and disappearing out the back of our contest.

I could see what he was doing, knew it was coming, yet fell for it every time as Burnsey used his skill to make an Aussie novice look a fool.

More often than not, we played with a tennis ball on a lined basketball court, with two school jumpers at each end of the pitch to determine the width of the goals. School shoes were shredded each and every term, my mother mystified as to what in the world was going on in the daylight hours. To say the matches were feisty is the understatement of the century.

Immediately after the bell rang for breaks, sprints to the canteen were followed by a brisk consumption of potentially the most wonderful of all school lunches. A sausage roll encased in a bread roll smothered with an excessive amount of sauce took little longer than two or three minutes to be demolished and only then could the football match begin.

Those lunchtime contests were the first experiences I had playing the game competitively. As a result, the passion shown may well have crossed the line of appropriateness on numerous occasions and I apologise sincerely to all those more level-headed and experienced players who I brought down recklessly.

To say a fire was lit is an understatement.

The more I played, watched and observed the game, the more compelling it became. The patience required, the euphoria and eruption around goals and the damp, cold and often snowy conditions in which football was played in a faraway land all drew me in.

Living opposite Salmon Reserve, a rectangular park blessed with ample space to enjoy outdoor activities, meant copious amounts of time spent playing with local kids. Touch football was frequently played, with rugby league the dominant and most popular sport in the area.

We played each afternoon, till dusk, before being beckoned inside by our mothers as dinner approached. Yet it was a group of older boys from a few streets away that appeared on Saturday afternoons and most fascinated me.

They seemed to appear magically, like the baseball players that emerged from the cornfields in the 1986 film *Field of Dreams*, mystically taking their places on the pitch and warming up. With the house so quiet, I always heard them before seeing them.

Greeks mostly, with a few Italians and Lebanese thrown in, they played football for hours and I sat on my front step about 80 metres away, never invited due to my age and correctly perceived lack of ability.

On one occasion, a rather extravagant clearing kick saw the sphere leave the playing surface, trundle down a small decline, cross the kerb of the road and roll towards my front lawn. A gigantically tall Greek boy I knew from school sprinted after it and I quickly realised that it was destined to reach me before he would catch up with it.

I left the front step, trotted across the lawn and gathered the old leather ball alongside my letterbox. He stopped in the middle of the road, gesturing for me to return the ball to him.

I paused for a moment, praying that he would ask, "Do you want to play?", "Do you like football?" or "Do you want to join in?"

Sadly, he didn't and I tossed the ball in his direction. They weren't to know, but a willing and probably easily defeated player had been lost to their game.

They played like champions, or so I thought, and their knowledge of the game was impressive. They shouted terms like Olympic and Marconi and knew names like Marshall Soper, John Kosmina and Peter Raskopoulos.

I frantically tried to learn the language and in a more digital age would have had far more success. But I struggled and, in the short term, the game was to remain something of a hidden, distant and yet to be fully understood passion.

With the clubs in the then National Soccer League divided along ethnic and cultural lines, I found it near impossible to access the domestic competition. My parents' discouragement had made it abundantly clear that, in their opinion, those fans in attendance were violent thugs. Thus, attending a game was an impossibility. Media coverage was mostly non-existent.

Combined with the fact that I had no money to pay for admission to matches and was also without the means to travel to and from them, the chances of attending were less than zero, barring a willing parent seeking to encourage my interest.

I had two parents and can assure you they were far from willing.

I would have loved to have collected cards with images of the local football stars, as I did of their league counterparts. Perhaps that could have led to an enhanced sense of connectedness with the game that these quick-talking, fast-footed youngsters were schooling me in each weekend.

Some early collections were printed in the 1970s before being discontinued, no doubt due to a lack of sales and/or interest. Even had they been deemed worthy to continue, they would most likely have been unavailable in my rugby league-centric area.

As time passed, I continued to follow West Ham's ladder fortunes in the newspaper, praying for wins to escape the dreaded drop, something I still do to this very day. The government-owned Special Broadcasting Service's commitment to football became apparent to me after rather dangerously daring to tune the box into the 'wog channel', as it was referred to in my home, one Sunday afternoon.

The early coverage is all a bit of a haze, yet bizarrely, Heidelberg goalkeeper Jeff Olver was my favourite of all the players I saw during that time period. The World Football program with Les Murray as host became something of an obsession, usually watched on an old 18-inch black-and-white television whilst wedged up against the back of my bedroom door.

Every now and then I would be 'busted', quickly claiming that there was nothing else to really watch and that I was "just having a quick look". Somehow it always worked, the television was permitted to stay and Les' magnificent knowledge and pronunciations, as well as the exotic nature of the matches the program featured, remained a possibility the following weekend.

It was around that point in time, 1986, I think, that school sport in Sydney underwent a cultural change.

In a rather controversial and shock move, my traditional and very Catholic secondary school began fielding a football team. It was unheard of, yet logical in another sense, as more and more young boys ceased participating in rugby league and began playing football at local clubs on weekends.

Around the same time, I befriended a young English boy named Thomas. He was a neat footballer, possessed all the best football lingo and jargon, had a ripping Birmingham accent, and they combined to dial up my interest in the game further.

Thomas played very competently on the left wing and encouraged me to attend open trials for the school's inaugural First XI, something for which we were mocked and jeered by many of our supposed mates. Both in Year 9 at the time, the expectation was that the majority of the squad would rightfully be made up of the more physically mature Year 10s.

We travelled by bus and I trembled the entire way, surrounded by boys who possessed boots and not Dunlop Volleys.

Asked which position I intended to play, I peered towards Thomas, begging for instruction. He was no help. All he could mutter was "Back". A note was made of that and, mercifully, the second half was slated for my debut appearance in a serious game of football.

What happened in that first half is a mystery, so nervous I was on the sideline, with the speed of the game instilling immense fear as to how on earth I would be able to keep up with it when I finally made it onto the pitch.

As the whistle blew to signify the start of the second period of play, I found myself stationed at left back, as a right footer and bereft of any idea as to how to defend, play out from defence or work the off-side trap.

What I did have was speed and any ball played in behind proved little trouble, as I was able to sweep it away across the sideline right-footed after a brief touch with my very weak left. My confidence grew.

As a poorly played pass trickled through to me on my left side and an opponent bore down just a handful of metres away, it occurred to me that the ball needed to be cleared, decisively and immediately. Some distance from the sideline and with only the left foot as an option, it was a now-or-never situation.

The generation of the power required to return it towards whence it came or hoof the ball over the sideline with my non-preferred foot became an issue. Somehow and in an absolute panic I crafted the best clearance I could from a standing start and with limited balance.

There was little distance to the kick; it travelled less than 30 metres, yet it did find the feet of Thomas who had slipped back into midfield at the time.

He turned on a dime and took the ball upfield with speed. It was a fluke of enormous proportions, but it must have appeared intentional to those observing.

I distinctly remember looking towards the sideline and spotting the selector/soon-to-be coach peering in my direction and making a small mark on the page in his clipboard.

Had I fooled them? You bet I had.

I played my first season of football with boys 12 months older than me, apart from Thomas who was one of the first selected. Honestly, I had little (or no) fucking idea what in the world I was doing!

Right back became my spot and I did okay, relying more on speed than skill and hoofing the ball clear rather than attempting to do anything that involved any intricacy or actual talent. The coach encouraged such an approach. He was a smart coach!

True to form, the secret was kept from my parents. They had no idea that for two entire seasons I was playing football and loving it, despite still developing my rather limited skills.

If there was a permission slip requiring signing, I must have forged it, because it was never presented to them. I do recall an awkward conversation or two when certain team photos appeared and my ugly mug was standing there in the back row. Passing the shots off as some sort of inter-school activity appeared to work and the only disappointment in the entire experience was a grand final loss in the second year, where I spent the entire 90 minutes on the pine.

If you thought this was going to be a heroic story of glory and triumph, you've obviously never seen me play.

There was no football during the final two years of school, undertaken at a new senior college that seemed more like a holiday camp than a place of learning. University had no such option either, yet the game grew deeper in my soul. Indoor soccer was a pretty popular endeavour at the time and the speed of it enhanced my skills a little, whilst I played casually in mixed teams in the early 2000s.

Side-tracked by professional concerns and a rather misguided and mostly ineffective pursuit of the opposite sex saw joining a local football club a lower priority, with the idea that there was always plenty of time to do so in the future bouncing around in the back of my head.

WHEN MUM AND DAD SEE ME KICK

Fortunately, I was surrounded by others with an equally strong passion for the game. We attended matches together and, slowly but surely, I became more aware of the way football was administrated and structured in Australia.

No doubt there were many moments where I could have taken the leap and committed to a team. Friends had made numerous offers to introduce me at their respective clubs, yet I had a nagging anxiety and uneasiness about encroaching on their turf. Despite a strong desire to become a part of their football lives, something always held me back.

Perhaps it was a fear of having less talent than required or a concern around fitting into a well-established culture and appearing the outsider. It certainly was not due to a lack of want.

I listened with envy when friends spoke of end-of-season trips away, the nicknames and idiosyncrasies of the other players, and the characters in their teams. I enjoyed watching them play, creeping ever closer to the inner circle, yet always at a distance that ensured any true feelings of belonging and community would remain just a little out of reach.

In retrospect, the failure to become part of a football-playing community is one of my very few regrets in life. Knowing now that many of the players I came to know socially had in fact enquired on multiple occasions whether I might like to join the team only inflames that regret.

Football clubs build wonderful, life-changing and life-lasting relationships, forged from a foundational home base that involves the simple act of kicking a ball between friends. Whilst some sense of satisfaction can be nurtured through informal play, the familiarity, comfort and collegiality found in organised teams and competitions cannot be fully replicated elsewhere.

Even with only limited experiences in such settings, it is a fact that grows ever clearer to me the longer I spend in and around football.

Perhaps not playing the game officially until I was 15 and missing out on those grounding experiences as a small child hampered the journey. I was left never quite feeling comfortable in my skin on a football pitch. However, with the intention and hope of playing the game formally in my 20s and a constant craving for a sense of community that family life had never provided, a flicker of possibility always remained.

Yet somewhere near the end of my third decade I was married, soon after a father and the quietly held football ambitions were soon jettisoned without ever really seeing the light of day.

The family and work life sonata began and there was little time for anything else. Having played golf for much of my life, a brisk 18 holes on a Saturday morning was the only realistic physical and emotional outlet possible. Slugging it out in one of the most under-appreciated professions—teaching—consumed many weeknights and weekends, with piles of paperwork needing immediate attention.

School teachers deserve medals, such are the demands of the job and the thankless nature of it.

Somehow, I managed it for 18 years. Frankly, it is something of a blur in retrospect. Thousands of students, examinations, assemblies and lessons all remain vivid, yet also merge into a collective memory. It is a recollection summarised by the frustrations and challenges of attempting to convey the wonders of the written word to mostly ambivalent students.

Much happened in the football world during those years in the classroom. The Socceroos qualified for the World Cup for the first time in 32 years. I can still recall almost breaking my hand on a wooden coffee table in a small North Strathfield unit in Sydney the moment John Aloisi converted his penalty kick against Uruguay on that brilliant November evening.

Aside from the joy that family brings, I am not too sure I have ever been happier in my life.

Around the same time and after the sad but inevitable destruction of the National Soccer League competition, the newly branded A-League began. New teams, colours and rivalries were born in 2005/06. Despite periods of treading water and disappointment, as some fell by the wayside in the early years, it remains something far better than anything we have ever seen in Australia in terms of broad reach and a sustainable top tier of professional football.

The game existed in the background of life when my kids were born in 2003 and 2007. As most parents can attest, those early years of child-rearing see many of the pleasures of adulthood pushed well and truly to one side. As such, football became something of an afterthought during that time.

With children tucked away in bed, there was potentially scope for some football viewing, yet with a spouse as educationally committed and tired as I was, it seemed particularly unfair to plonk down in front of the box and watch a sporting contest in which she had absolutely no interest.

More often than not, we watched some light comedy with perhaps a bit of late-night English Premier League to follow, as she quietly slept on the lounge alongside me.

Every now and then a rare A-League game fell in the perfect window. Perhaps the children were napping, at a party, or better yet, occupied with something else that kept them away from the lounge room. However, I watched less football than I ever had during that period and would guess that many other parents have experienced the same.

Seeing my mature and successful daughters now in young adulthood confirms that it was time well spent and a sacrifice worth making. Yet it is also nice to have the television back on my terms.

With the drain of teaching wearing me down more quickly than ever before, I was looking for something else. Exactly what it was, I had utterly no idea. However, it did seem clear that there MUST be something else, another path, another way, another direction.

By chance, I made casual contact with a person passionate about football and, as I was to discover a little later on, involved in the media coverage of it.

That was in 2014 and, at first, I thought little of it. Contributing to a few websites and dabbling in some radio work, they had apparently spent a lifetime in the game, knew it well, and supplemented a full-time job with writing and speaking about Australia's domestic scene.

On a stinking hot summer night in December 2014, I sat down and Googled the name of a website to which they contributed. I located a recent piece and read it.

The decision to do so was to change my life.

On an equally sweaty December afternoon just a few days later, I wrote my first ever article for a website to which I still contribute today. Recently I re-read the copy and whilst containing raw elements of unprofessionalism, it did speak some truth.

The piece was submitted late in the evening and as the sub-editors went to work on the first submission from a new, amateur writer of whom they had no previous knowledge, I eagerly awaited its publication.

That occurred the following morning and the buzz of seeing my own work in print addicted me in an instant. It was also the trigger that helped form an idea in my head to once and for all escape from the trappings of the classroom and do something far more satisfying and rewarding.

Completely addicted to the idea of writing about sport, I went ballistic, knocking out three or four pieces a week. Most were football focused, but tennis, rugby league, Australian Rules football and cricket were also on my radar. As less and less attention went towards lesson plans and academic programs, I produced more and more content.

Of course, not a dollar was earned, but it mattered little. The sheer thrill of expressing clear ideas about the issues in football and the ensuing online debate created an intellectual sustenance that I had not experienced before.

I had always told my kids, "Work out what you love doing and find a way to get paid for it!"

Those words were ringing in my ears as I wondered whether there was any future in the new endeavour.

Two and a half years later, I tapped the Gmail application on my mobile phone as I sat at the intersection of the M2 Motorway and the always busy Windsor Road, in the north west of Sydney. A curious message appeared from one of the editors of the website.

In short, it was an offer to write for them on a paid basis, with two articles per week and a modest reimbursement mentioned. I sat patiently at the lights, crying like a baby, so proud and humbled all at the same time.

My youngest is a sharp thinker. After being told the news later that night, she intuitively said, "That is what you have been working towards, Dad."

That moment set me on a path that has led directly to this book.

The journey that followed has involved the privilege of being asked to contribute to an array of publications over the last eight years, hundreds of live blogs of football matches from right around the globe at sometimes the most inconvenient of hours, and a lessening in earnings that my patient wife faced with only calm and support.

My best guess is that at the time of writing, I have compiled in excess of three thousand articles and around 2.4 million words on the beautiful game. I have written on everything from the triumphant 2015 Asian Cup won by Ange Postecoglou's Socceroos, to the 2018 and 2022 FIFA Men's World Cups, the Women's World Cup in France in 2021, and season upon season of A-League play that provides the unexpected and dramatic year on year.

Somewhere in the middle of all that business and me being unlikely to lace up a pair of boots and play the game with my often aching and creaking body, it occurs to me that a space of belonging and community within the game has been found in what was the most unexpected of ways.

If only I had known that arriving at such a space need not necessarily involve kicking a ball. Rather accidentally, I stumbled into the always accepting arms of football as a writer, a commentator and now author.

Football has done something similar for each of the subjects in this book.

It is that universality and the ability of football to invite all and sundry to its table, in spite of difference, that enunciates the clear fact that no one story is more valuable, more compelling or more important than another.

Nor should how long someone has spent on a pitch or walked the sidelines as a coach or manager—nor the country from whence they hail—have any impact on the inherent value of their place within football. Irrespective of the back story we all have, each and every person who worships the sphere and the complete global phenomena it has become brings something unique to it.

That personal contribution is based on life experiences from all corners of the globe, experiences that provide the diversity within and the essential fabric of the game.

The stories in this book prove that fact in spades, with each subject equally important and educative when it comes to an understanding of the game and all its beauty and challenges. As a collective, we form the 'football community'. These are potentially two of the most powerful words on the planet.

Some of us will be superb players, others masterful tacticians and the vast majority, enthusiastic and passionate observers and fans. Others will administrate the game, work at a grass-roots level or perhaps even take to writing about it.

United, we provide a place of security and belonging, and potentially exist as an instructive metaphor from which our planet could learn a great deal.

I am so pleased to have ended up as a part of the world's largest community. Like many others, the journey to get here was not a streamlined or expected one, with twists and turns and humps and bumps along the way, before eventually arriving in a contented place.

Writing colleagues, radio broadcasters who kindly ask me to appear on their programs and the publishers who support my work have all contributed to those feelings of contentment. It is a case in point that clearly proves the fact that football possesses a power to take human beings to places they never felt possible.

It brought me to a new career within the game, despite the fact that early on, such an opportunity seemed highly unlikely.

After all, Mum and Dad never even saw me kick.

ACKNOWLEDGEMENTS

Some people find it difficult to talk to others. I don't. Frankly, I think we live in an often cold world, as people hustle and bustle in a million directions, never really getting anywhere, with most happy to tread on a few faces along the way.

I've always tried to be a little better than that, despite failing on numerous occasions and I still believe that a more perfect version of humanity is realistically possible. As I've carried my knapsack through life and consumed sport at what most would describe as an unhealthy rate, meeting hundreds of memorable people who love and embrace the game of football has been nothing but a sheer joy.

The odd old fella in a sweaty and stinky bar, a mum and dad watching their tyro from the stands or a troubled youth for whom the game has provided so much, have all stumbled across my path at different stages. I've met good players, great players, terrible players, crazy players, angry parents, deranged officials and just about everyone from the most clever football academic to the silliest fan and enjoyed every single one of those conversations.

To all of them, I say thank you. Mostly, the conversations appeared to have given people joy in the retelling of them, often jettisoning some baggage and sometimes even forging friendships that continue to this day. Without the people who showed me a trust and belief that others haven't, this book would be nothing but a hazy idea. I hope you enjoy seeing your lived experience in words.

The notion of exploring how football means so many different things to so many different people, was originally an off the cuff comment in an Email to Bonita Mersiades, the editor-in-chief at Fair Play Publishing. It was Bonita who nudged me in terms of potentially formalising the idea. Without one of football's greatest supporters, this book may not exist and to Bonita, thank you for your never ending encouragement and support.

Of course, writing this book, the others in the works and the mountain of copy that I file each week to make a living, means odd hours and nothing like a nine-to-five schedule. To my glamorous wife who backed my writing journey when I checked out of teaching in 2017 and my two amazing children Lauryn and Sarah, I say thank you, even though it would take far more than two simple words to express how much I thrive on your love and energy.

ABOUT THE AUTHOR

After 20 years working in the education sector, Stuart Thomas began writing for **TheRoar.com.au** in 2015. Covering football, rugby league, cricket, tennis, rugby union and AFL, his articles have subsequently featured across an array of websites and publications, including Play On magazine and **zerodigital.com.au**.

Living in Sydney, Australia with his partner and two teenage children, Stuart also works in sub-editing, blogs sporting events live, and runs a successful nursery in the north-west of Sydney. *When Mum and Dad See Me Kick* is his first book.

More really good football books from Fair Play Publishing

Encyclopedia of Socceroos
Centenary Edition

Burning Ambition
The Centenary of Australia-New Zealand Football Ashes

Whatever It Takes
The Inside Story of the FIFA Way

Coming Soon

Encyclopedia of Matildas
World Cup Edition

"Get Your Tits Out
For The Lads"

Hell For Leather
The World of a Sporting Journalist

fairplaypublishing.co.au/shop

www.ingramcontent.com/pod-product-compliance
Lightning Source LLC
Chambersburg PA
CBHW072059110526
44590CB00018B/3240